Elements of Rasāyana Therapy in Āyurveda

Indian Medical Science Series No. 133

Elements of Rasāyana Therapy in Āyurveda

PROF. AJAY KUMAR SHARMA

Sri Satguru Publications
A Division of
Indian Books Centre
Delhi, India

Published by
Sri Satguru Publications,
Indological and Oriental Publishers
A Division of
Indian Books Centre
40/5, Shakti Nagar,
Delhi-110007
India

Website : http://www.indianbookscentre.com
email : ibcindia@vsnl.com

First Edition: Delhi, 2005

ISBN 81-7030-831-3

Printed at Chawla Offset Printers, Delhi 110 052

Dedication

Lord Ganeśa

Dedicated

to

My Revered Parents (Late) Shri Shyam Lal Sharma and Smt. Bimla Devi Sharma who had always inspired me to work for helping the suffering humanity.

Whatever I have achieved uptil now is the result of sacrifices, devotion, sincerity, pains & discomforts born by my dear parents in bringing me up. I am extremely lucky to have such ideal parents. May God bless & inspire me to work for the fulfillment of the dreams of my caring & loving parents especially helping the needy.

Prof. Ajay Kumar Sharma

CONTENTS

Foreword

It was a pleasure to go through the press script of the book **"Elements of *Rasāyana* Therapy in *Āyurveda*"** authored by Prof. A.K. Sharma. The book has made a good attempt to review the classical concepts and contemporary status of *Rasāyana* therapy in a simplified style making a good reading for readers of today. The book, besides general introduction, deliberates scholarly on the historical aspects of the subject, Basic concepts of *Rasāyana* therapy and its applications, Biological effects of *Rasāyana* remedies, concept of Aging in *Āyurveda* and Anti-Aging impact of *Rasāyana* besides specific descriptions of *Rasāyana* in *Brihattrayī* texts. The book provides a comprehensive bibliography and opens avenues for further reading. I have gathered the impression that the able author has done a good piece of work and has succeeded to make a notable addition to the contemporary *Āyurvedic* literature.

I have known the author Prof. A.K. Sharma as a scholar and an activist in the field of *Āyurveda* with scientific temper for many years besides reading his other books specially the one on *Panca Karma* therapy written on similar style which has already been accepted well by the contemporary readers. I wish a good success for the present publication too.

Rasāyana Therapy is one of the most prominent components of *Āyurvedic* medicine. *Āyurveda*, the Science of Life, has two fold objectives, 1. To preserve and promote the health of the healthy and 2. To alleviate the illness of the sick. Thus it has a dual role encompassing both "the health" and "the disease". Out of the two the former has been given greater significance than the latter. *Āyurveda* deliberates extensively on the approaches and the methods of preventive and promotive health care. The entire range of *Swastha Vritta, Sada Vritta, Acāra, Āhara-Vihāra* and the rejuvenative measures of *Rasāyana Tantra* have been developed since antiquity for promotion of health and prevention of diseases. Periodical bio-purification through *Panca Karma* therapy and multi-dimensional promotion of health through *Rasāyana* therapy form the central theme of promotive health care in *Āyurveda*. The present monograph deals with the subject, which is of paramount importance.

The *Rasāyana* therapy has been described in all classical texts of *Āyurveda*, both in *Brihattrayis* and *Laghuttrayis*. The *Carak Samhitā* which is the foremost among the *Āyurvedic* classics describes *Rasāyana Tantra* in its very first chapter of *Cikitsā Sthāna* elaborately devided into four *Pādās,* where a detailed account of the fundamental concepts of *Rasāyana* therapy, its variants and methodologies of use are described alongwith the mention of a range of *Rasāyana* remedies, both single and compound including the popular recipe *Cyawanprāśa*. *Suśruta Samhitā* which is the second most important classical treatise, does not describe *Rasāyana* therapy in the beginning of *Cikitsā Sthāna*, rather it postpones the subject towards the end of *Cikitsā Sthāna* while *Vāgbhatta* minimizes the description only in a one small chapter that too, towards the end of the *Samhitā* i.e. in the last but one chapter of *Uttara Tantra*. Such a placing of the sequence of descriptions may be because of many other reasons but it could also reflect the fact that probably the importance of this great science had started declining in its significance even in the *Samhitā* period itself probably because of growing supremacy of curative medicine over preventive medicine.

The term *Rasāyana (Rasa + Ayana)* essentially refers to nutrition and nourishment. More specifically it refers to bioavailability of nutrition. There can be many mechanisms through which a *Rasāyana* remedy may accelerate the phenomenon of nourishment. Logically it seems that a *Rasāyana* may act at three levels of bio-system to promote nutrition such as 1. At the level of *Agni* by promoting the digestion and metabolism, 2. At the level of *Srotasa* by promoting the microcirculation and tissue perfusion and 3. At the level of *Rasa* itself by acting as direct nutrition. Thus the *Rasāyana* remedies act essentially on nutrition dynamics and rejuvenate the body and psyche. They are the powerful means of promotion of health, longevity and prevention of diseases. They sustain the *Ojas Status* and *Bala* in the body and promote *Vyādhiksamatva* i.e. Immunity. Many *Rasāyana* drugs of *Āyurveda* have been recently demonstrated to possess immuno-enhancer activity when tested on scientific parameters.

In this context it cannot be overemphasized that Genetics and Immunology were highly developed branches of knowledge in ancient times which is evident from descriptions available in *Āyurvedic* classics which appear not only strikingly similar to latest modern knowledge on the subject today, rather many ancient concepts display significant supremacy and open newer vistas for future development.

Āyurveda propounds the concept of *Ojas* describing it as the quintessence of all *Dhātus* which is responsible for *Bala* i.e. immunity or biological strength to resist a disease both physical and mental including microbial, metabolic and stress-related ones. The *Rasāyanās* are the enhancers of *Ojas* and *Bala* and hence form the most important component of therapeutics. *Bala* i.e. Immunity is of three categories—"त्रिविधं बलं सहजं कालजं युक्ति कृतं च।" -1. *Sahaja* i.e. inherent natural immunity, 2. *Kālaja* i.e. immunity which is imparted spontaneously by influence of *Kāla* i.e. time *viz.* climate, season, age etc. 3. *Yuktikṛta* i.e. the acquired immunity which can be obtained by artificial means i.e. planned artificial therapeutic immuno-enhancing. This knowledge, which is thousands of years old, is as modern as modern science of today, rather it has rich futuristic scope of development.

The ancients also deliberated very precisely on the nature of immune disorders—"त्रय दोषा बलस्योक्ता" i.e. Immune disorders may be basically of three categories—*Oja Vyāpata, Oja Visransa, Oja Kṣaya.* It so scientifically depicts the early and reversible immuno aberration, dislodgement of immunity like autoimmune disorders and real immuno deficiency. There are also methods to rectify these disorders. The *Sansodhana* therapy of *Panca Karma* and *Rasāyana* therapy appear to play fundamental role in the management of such disorders.

Prof. Ram Harsh Singh

Vice Chancellor
Rajasthan Āyurveda University, Jodhpur
Formerly Professor-Head Kāyacikitsā and
Dean, Faculty of Ayurveda
Banaras Hindu University, Varanasi.

Jodhpur,
31st may, 2004

Acknowledgements

I wish to express my deep gratitude and indebtness to **Prof. R.H. Singh, Vice Chancellor, Rajasthan Āyurveda University, Jodhpur,** my revered benevolent teacher, an eminent scholar of *Āyurveda* and internationally accalimed Scientist for his inspiring and constant encouragements. Prof. Singh, a noted scholar of *Āyurveda* has written the "Foreword" for this book for which the author is grateful. Prof. Singh has done commendable work on scientific parameters in the field of *Rasāyana* which has opened newer vistas in this field for future research works.

I was greatly inspired to work in this field by my senior colleague **Prof. B.L. Gaur, Director, National Institute of Āyurveda, Jaipur,** to whom I am grateful.

In preparation of this monograph I have received invaluable help from my Post Graduate Students especially Mr. Avinash Jain, Miss Seema Bhadora, Mr. Rajesh Gupta and Mr. Gaurish Gupta to whom I wish to convey my thanks.

With profound reverence, appeciation and affection I wish to express my deep gratitude to my father (Late) Sh. S.L. Sharma, my mother Smt. Bimla Devi, my elder brother Mr. Ashok Kumar Sharma, my sister in law Smt. Neelima Sharma, my brother in law Dr. Y.N. Sharma 'Arun' and my elder sister Smt. Asha Sharma and all my friends and colleagues for their constant inspirations and blessings for completion of this work.

It is my humble desire to express my deep gratitude and indebtness to my wife Dr. (Smt.) Praveen Sharma, the main source of my inspiration and strength, my son Amit Sharma and my daughter Gauri Sharma for their love and support (without which this book could have never been completed) manifested in several ways but in particular through their patience and understanding.

Lastly, I Wish to acknowledge my obligations and sincere thanks to Mr. Sunil Gupta, my publishers M/s Indian Books Centre, 40/5 Shakti Nagar, Delhi-110007 (India) for his splendid cooperation and for printing the books so nicely and in time.

Jaipur, **AJAY KUMAR SHARMA**
31st May, 2004

Preface

Āyurveda is one of the world's oldest system of health. It is not just a health care system but a complex approach to healthy living. *Āyurveda* is the science of life which has two objectives, to maintain & promote the positive health of healthy individuals and to cure the disease of diseased ones. *Āyurveda* is practiced in the form of *Aṣṭānga Āyurveda* (Eight Fold *Āyurveda*) which includes *Śalya* (Surgery), *Śālākya* (E.N.T.), *Kāyacikitsā* (General Medicine), *Kaumāra Bhṛtya* (Pediatrics), *Agada Tantra* (Juriceprudence & Toxicology), *Bhūtavidyā* (science dealing with Devils), *Rasāyana* (Geriatrics) and *Vājikaraṇa* (Virity promoters).

More emphasis is laid down on health promotive measures i.e. preventive aspects of a disease in *Āyurveda*. This is possible by improving the resistance of the body against the diseases i.e. by improving Immunity of the body. This could be achieved with the administration of *"Rasāyana"* i.e. Geriatrics or Immunomodulator drugs. The term *"Rasāyana"* means the ways of attaining excellent *Rasa Dhātu* which rejuvenates all body tissues and prevents premature aging and diseases. Healthful longevity has ever been cherished desire of man. *Rasāyana* is one of the eight clinical specialties of classical *Āyurveda*. *Rasāyana* is not only a drug therapy but a specialized procedure practiced in the form of rejuvenating recipe, dietary regimen and special health promoting conduct and behaviour i.e. *Ācāra Rasāyana*.

While describing the properties of *Rasāyana, Ācārya Caraka* has mentioned that on administration of *Rasāyana* one attains longevity, memory, intelligence, freedom from diseases, youthful age, excellence of lusture, complexion and voice, respectability and brilliance. *Ācārya Suśruta* has clearly stated that *Rasāyana* drugs are "*Urjaskara*" in nature and they prevent diseases and old age.

Ācārya Caraka has given great importance to *Rasāyana Tantra* by devoting first chapter of *Cikitsā Sthāna* to *Rasāyana* which has four *Pādās* (Subchapters) describing various principles of *Rasāyana* Therapy. While in *Suśruta Samhitā,* it is described in chapters 27-29 of *Cikitsā Sthāna* and in *Aṣṭānga Hṛdya* of *Vāgabhaṭṭa* it is not described in *Cikitsā Sthāna* but is described briefly in the last but one chapter of *Uttarsthāna*. This reflects on the declining impact of *Rasāyana* Therapy in *Samhitā* period. But lately *Rasāyana* Therapy is attracting lot of attention globally in the form of rejuvenation and geriatric care. It has been proved scientifically that most of the *Rasāyana* drugs are antistress and adaptogenic in nature besides having Immunomodulating effects. These drugs promote quality of life and reduce the rate of aging.

My post graduate students have been inspiring me to bring out a book on *Rasāyana* Therapy in English covering all literary review along with latest developments in the concerned field. I am happy to present this book on "**Elements of *Rasāyana* Therapy in *Āyurveda***" to the prospective readers. It is hoped that this book will interest the Students, Teachers, Researchers and practitioners of *Āyurveda*. In this book the author has tried to compile the Classical Concepts about *Rasāyana* Therapy available in various *Āyurvedic* Texts by rearranging the subject matter systematically in more practicable form. The book reviews the ancient classical concepts and recent advances made in this important field of Gerontology.

The book contains nine chapters. First two chapters deal with the general introduction and Historical review of *Rasāyana* Therapy in various Treaties of *Āyurveda.* Third chapter deals with the exhaustive description of *Rasāyana Tantra* in various *Samhitās* of *Āyurveda.* Biological effects of *Rasāyana* Drugs are described in fourth chapter. *Āyurvedic* Concept of Aging (*Jarā*) and its prevention with *Rasāyana* is described in fifth chapter. Chapter Nos. Sixth, Seventh, Eighth and Ninth deal with description of *Rasāyana* in *Caraka, Suśruta, Aṣṭānga Sangraha* and *Aṣṭānga Hṛdya* respectively. A bibliography of references is appended in the end in chapter no. 10. All the topics have been written with emphasis on the uniqueness and distinction of *Āyurvedic* concepts with an attempt to evaluate the relevance and validity of the same in modern times. The author has utilized his professional experience with clinical Medicine of *Āyurveda* in compiling the present work.

Opinions and suggestions to improve the book are welcome.

Jaipur, **AJAY KUMAR SHARMA**

31st May, 2004

Chapter I

General Introduction

Āyurveda is the science of life which has following two main objectives—

1. To maintain and promote the positive health of healthy individuals.
2. To cure the disease of diseased ones.

Āyurveda deals with various aspects of healthy living and various remedies to be adopted in diseased conditions. *Āyurveda* is one of the world's oldest systems of health. It is not just a health care system but a complete approach to healthy living.

Āyurveda is practised in the form of *Aṣṭāṅga Āyurveda*[1] today which is divided into following eight branches—

1. *Śalya* (Surgery)
2. *Śālākya* (E.N.T.)
3. *Kāyacikitsā* (General Medicine)
4. *Kaumāra Bhṛtya* (Paediatrics)
5. *Agada Tantra* (Jurice Prudence and Toxicology)

---

१. तद्यथा-शल्यं, शालाक्यं, कायचिकित्सा, भूतविद्या, कौमारभृत्यम्, अगद तन्त्रं, रसायन तन्त्रं, वाजीकरण तन्त्रमिति।।

(सुश्रुत-सूत्र स्थान-१/७)

6. *Bhūtavidyā* (Science dealing with Devils, Giants, Ghosts, Demons and Evil Spirits)
7. *Rasāyana* (Geriatrics)
8. *Vājīkaraṇa* (Aphrodisiacs, Virility Promoters)

More emphasis is laid down over the promotion and maintenance of positive health of masses according to principles of *Āyurveda*. A long healthy life has been the cherished desire of man since antiquity. *Rasāyana*, one of the eight clinical specialities of classical *Āyurveda* is an important speciality aiming at rejuvenation and geriatric care.

On the other hand if a person falls ill his disease is to be cured by administrating him adequate *cikitsā* (treatment). The term *cikitsā* refers to the treatment of a disease or ailment afflicting an individual in mental and physical dimensions. Controlled Diet (*Āhāra*), specific life styie (*Vihāra*) and appropriate *Bhaiṣja* (*Auṣadhi*-Medicine) are essential components of an ideal *cikitsā* for curing a particular disease.

Bheṣaja **(Medicine-Therapeutics)**

All the *Dravyās* which are found in this world are *Bheṣaja*.[1] Judicious use of various *Dravyās* in various forms can be used in various conditions to achieve the objective of curing the diseases of masses. Thus all the *Dravyās* when used with specific approach, for a specific purpose in a specific condition act as *Auṣadha* (Medicine).

---

१. अनेनोपदेशेन नानौषधीभूतं जगति किञ्चिद् द्रव्यमुपलभ्यते तां तां युक्तिमर्थं च तं तमभिप्रेत्य।।

(चरक सूत्र २६/१२)

(सुश्रुत सूत्र ४१/८)

Ācārya Vāgabhatta has clearly stated that all the *Dravyās* have *Pānca Bhautika* composition[1] i.e. all the *Dravyās* are made up of *Panca Mahābhūtās* viz. *Pṛthvi, Jala, Teja, Vāyu* and *Ākāsa*. Depending on their clinical utility the *Ausadha Dravyās* are divided into two groups—

1. ***Auṣadha Bhūta* or *Hitakara* or *Pathya***—These type of *Auṣadha Dravyās* are of great importance as these are useful for our body. These *Dravyās* when used judiciously may induce 'Acquired Immunity' in the body, besides alleviating various disorders.

2. ***Anauṣadha Bhūta* or *Ahitakara* or *Apathya***—These group of *Auṣadha Dravyās* are harmful for the body as these may precipitate or aggravate the underlying disorders in the body on their administration. These drugs possess various side and toxic effects.

Auṣadhi (Medicine)

A substance or material or *dravya* which alleviates the pain or agony is termed as *Auṣadhi* (medicine).[2] The word "*Auṣa*" means '*Rasa*', thus *Auṣadhi* is that *dravya* which contains '*Rasa*' (Active principle).[3] In *Vedās* the word '*Mātā*' is substituted for the word *Auṣadhi* (Medicine).[4] *Ācārya Gangādhara* has stated that *Auṣadhi*

---

१. इह हि द्रव्यं पञ्चमहाभूतात्मकम्। तस्याधिष्ठानं पृथिवी, योनिरूदकं खानिलानलसमवायान्निर्वृत्तिविशेषौ। उत्कर्षेण तु व्यपदेशः।
(अष्टांग संग्रह सूत्र स्थान-१७/३)

२. औषधं रूजं धयति इति औषधि।

३. ओषो नाम रसः सोऽस्यां धीयते इति औषधिः।

४. औषधीरिति मातरस्तद्वो देवीरूप ब्रुवे। (ऋग्वेद १०/९०/४)

are beneficial in various diseases.[1] In *Nirukta Nighantu*[2] the word '*Auṣadhi*' has been used in reference to a substance which provides nutrition to the body. Thus, on administration *Auṣadhi* produces *Bala* (Vigour), *Śaktī* (Vitality) and *Oja* (Essence of all *Dhātūs*) in the body. The synonymous word *Bheṣaja* is also used for the word *Auṣadhi*.

Synonyms of *Bheṣaja* (Medicine-Therapeutics)

Ther term *Bheṣaja* signifies the measures used for overcoming the fear of occurrence of a disease.[3] Thus *Bheṣaja* can be defined to be the measures or *dravyās* used to control the diseases and to maintain the health of diseased persons.

Various terms have been used by *Ācārya Caraka* as synonyms to the term '*Bheṣaja*' having similar meanings,[4] which are described below—

1. ***Cikitsā***—That which alleviates disorders.
2. ***Vyādhihara***—Destroyer of diseases.
3. ***Pathya***—Beneficial for the channels (*Srotasa*).
4. ***Sādhana***—That which is instrument for performance.
5. ***Auṣadha***—That which is prepared by herbs.
6. ***Prāyaścitta***—Expiation, to make amendments or reparation for sin.

---

१. ओषधिभिर्निष्पन्नं व्याधिहितं, तदुपलक्षणत्वात् सर्वे चिकित्सतमौषध रूढम्। (गङ्गाधर)।

२. ओषः तेजो धीयते यत्र स औषधि। (निरुक्त निघण्टु)

३. भेषं रोगभयं जयति इति भेषजम्।

४. चिकित्सितं व्याधिहरं पथ्यं साधनमौषधम्।
प्रायश्चित्तं प्रशमनं प्रकृतिस्थापनं हितम्।
विद्याद्भेषजनामानि (चरक चिकित्सा-१/१/३)

7. ***Praśamana***—Pacification of Vitiated *Doṣās*.
8. ***Prakṛtisthāpana***—That which helps in recovery.
9. ***Hita***—Wholesome which are beneficial for the body.

Types of *Bheṣaja*

On the basis of their therapeutic effects, *Bheṣaja* is described to be of two types[1]—

1. ***Swathasyorjaskara***—That *Bheṣaja* which promotes strength and immunity in the healthy.

2. ***Roganuta* or *Rogaghna***—That *Bheṣaja* which alleviates various disorders.

That *Bheṣaja* which promotes strength and immunity, mostly in the healthy individuals, is usually included in *Vṛṣya* (Aphrodisiac) and *Rasāyana* (Rejuvenative and promotive treatment), while the *Bheṣaja* of the second group is mostly used for alleviation of disorders of different kinds. Although both the groups of medicines perform both the functions, but the medicines of first group are mostly used for promoting positive health by improving the immunity in the form of preventive and prophylactic medicine. On the other hand the medicines of second group are mainly used for alleviation of various disorders in the form of curative medicine.

With the administration of promotive treatment i.e. *Swasthasyorjaskara Bheṣaja*, one attains longevity, memory, intelligence, freedom from diseases, youthful age, excellence

---

१. भेषजं द्विविधं च तत्।
स्वस्थास्योर्जस्करं किञ्चित् किञ्चिदार्तस्य रोगनुत्।।
(चरक चिकित्सा-१/१/४)

of lusture, complexion and voice, optimum strength of physique and sense organs, successful words, respectability and brilliance. *Rasāyana* (promotive treatments) means the ways of attaining excellent *Rasa Dhātu* etc.[1,2]

Vājīkaraṇa (Aphrodisiac) treatment,[3] is that which produces lineage of progeny, quick sexual stimulation, enables one to perform sexual act with the women uninterruptedly and vigorously like a horse, makes one charming for the women, promotes corpulence, and infallible and indestructible semen even in the old persons, renders one great having a number of off-springs like a sacred tree branched profusely and commanding respect and popularity in the society. By this one attains eternality based on filial tradition here and hereafter along with fame, fortune, strength and corpulence.

---

१. दीर्घमायुः स्मृतिं मेधामारोग्यं तरुणं वयः।
प्रभा वर्णस्वरौदार्यं देहेन्द्रियबलं परम्।।
(चरक चिकित्सा-१/१/७)

२. वाक्सिद्धिं प्रणतिं कान्तिं लभते ना रसायनात्।
लाभोपायो हि शस्तानां रसादीनां रसायनम्।।
(चरक चिकित्सा-१/१/८)

३. अपत्य संतानकरं यत् सद्यः संप्रहर्षणम्।
वाजी वातिबलो येन यात्यप्रतिहतः स्त्रियः।।
भवत्यतिप्रियः स्त्रीणां येन येनो पचीयते।
जीर्यतोऽप्यक्षयं शुक्रं फल वद्येन दृश्यते।।
प्रभूतशाखः शाखीव येन चैत्यो यथा महान्।
भवत्यच्र्यो बहुमतः प्रजानां सुबहुप्रजः।।
संतान मूलं येनेह प्रेत्य चानन्त्यमश्नुते।
यशः श्रियं बलं पुष्टिं वाजीकरणमेव तत्।।
(चरक चिकित्सा-१/१/९-१२)

Thus *Swasthasyorsaskara Bheṣaja* is of two types[1]—

(i) ***Rasāyana***[2]—It means the ways of attaining excellent *Rasa Dhātu* which rejuvenates all body tissues.

(ii) ***Vājikaraṇa***[3]—It means the ways of enabling one to perform sexual act with the women as vigorously as a horse and which makes one charming for the women.

The basic difference between *Rasāyana* and *Vājikarṇa* is that the *Rasāyana* is used in a diseased or healthy persons for the purpose of attaining best quality of *Rasādi Dhātus* which rejuvenates all body tissues and thus produces strength and vitality in the body, where as *Vājikaraṇa* in addition to producing strength & vitality in the body leads to specific enhancement of sexual potency.

Roganuta or ***Rogaghna Bheṣaja***[4] is also of two types which primarily alleviates various disorders[5]—

1. ***Roga Praśamanakara***—It includes those medicines which on administration pacify vitiated *Doṣās* and thus control the diseases.

---

१. स्वस्थस्योर्जस्करं यत्तु तद् वृष्यं तद्रसायनम्।।
(चरक चिकित्सा-१/१/५)

२. लाभोपायो हि शस्तानां रसादीनां रसायनम्।
(चरक चिकित्सा-१/१/८)

३. येन नारीषु सामर्थ्यं वाजिवल्लभते नरः।
व्रजेच्चाभ्यधिकं येन वाजीकरणमेव तत्।।
(चरक चिकित्सा-२/४/५१)

४. प्रायः, प्रायेण रोगाणां द्वितीयं प्रशमे मतम्।
(चरक चिकित्सा-१/१/६)

५. रोगघ्नमपि द्विविधं रोगस्य प्रशमनपुनर्भवकरं च।
(अष्टाङ्ग संग्रह)

2. ***Apunarbhava***—In addition to arresting the progress of disease, these medicines prevent recurrence of that particular disease.

***Abheṣaja* (*Anauṣadha*)**

A *drayva* (drug) or *Karma* (actions) acting against *Bheṣaja* is termed as *Abheṣaja* or *Anauṣadha*. *Abheṣaja* is that which is contrary to therapy and therefore it should be avoided[1] as it may complicate the disease and may be fatal for the individual. *Abheṣaja* or *Anauṣadha* is also of two types[2]—

1. ***Bādhana***—It may lead to sudden death or may be extremely harmful for the body immediately just after administration in the body. It is acute in onset e.g. poisons.

2. ***Sānubādhana* or *Anubādhana***—It may lead to death of the individual in due course of time or may be fatal for the person after some time. It is chronic in onset e.g. *Dūṣi Viṣa*.

---

१. अभेषजमिति ज्ञेयं विपरीतं यदौषधात्।
(चरक चिकित्सा-१/१/१५)

२. अभेषजं च द्विविधं बाधनं सानुबाधनम्।
(चरक चिकित्सा-१/१/५)

Types of *Bheṣaja-Auṣadha*-Medicine

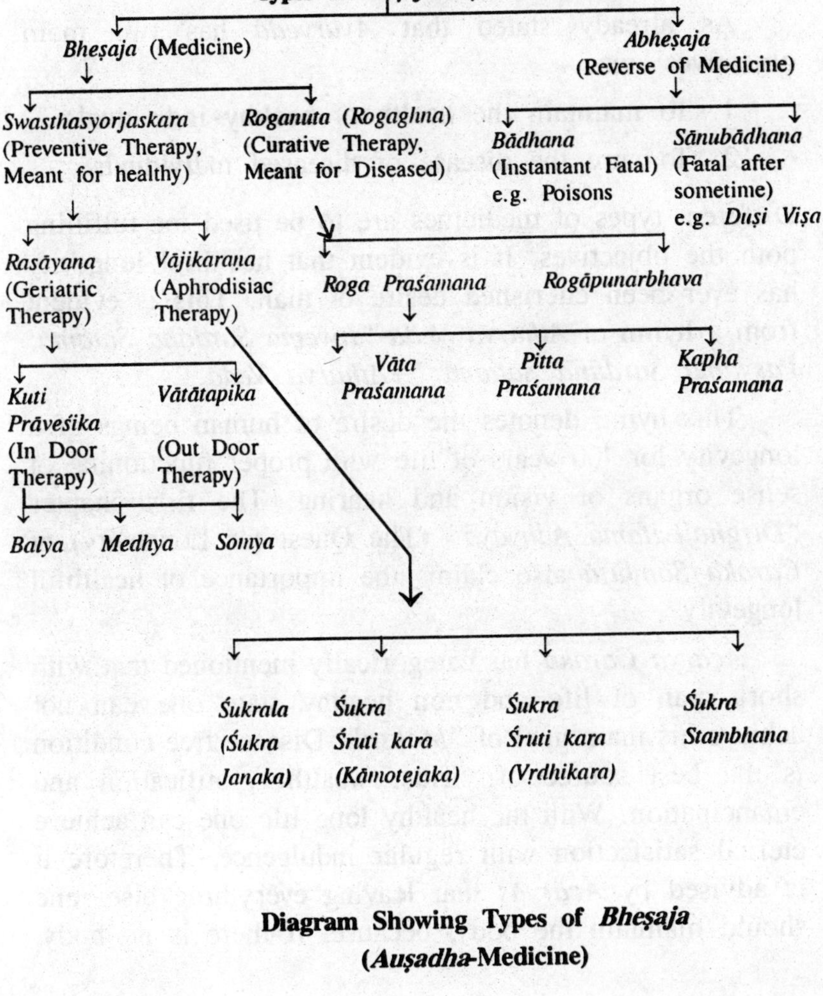

Diagram Showing Types of *Bheṣaja* (*Auṣadha*-Medicine)

Importance of *Rasāyana Tantra*

As already stated that *Āyurveda* has two main objectives[1] viz.—

1. To maintain the health of healthy individuals.
2. To cure the disease of diseased individuals.

Different types of medicines are to be used for fulfilling both the objectives. It is evident that healthful longevity has ever been cherished desire of man. This is evident from a hymn of *Atharva Veda-"Jīwema Śardaha Śatama, Pasyama Śardaha Śatama."–Atharva Veda*.

This hymn denotes the desire of human beings of a longevity for 100 years of life with proper functioning of sense organs of vision and hearing. The first chapter "*Dīrghajīvitama Adhyāya*" (The Quest for Longevity) of *Caraka Samhitā* also claims the importance of healthful longevity.

Ācārya Caraka has categorically mentioned that with short span of life and non healthy state one can not achieve his main goal of "*Mokṣa*"[2] Disease free condition is the best source of virtue, wealth, gratification and emancipation. With the healthy long life one can achieve eternal satisfaction with regular indulgence. Therefore it is advised by *Ācāryās* that leaving everything else, one should maintain the body, because, if there is no body,

---

१. प्रयोजनं चास्य स्वस्थस्य स्वास्थ्य रक्षणमातुरस्य विकार प्रशमनं च।
(चरक सूत्र ३०/२६)

२. धर्मार्थ काममोक्षाणां आरोग्य मूल मूत्तमम्॥
(चरक सूत्र-१/१५)

there is nothing that can be made available to the individual.[1]

A wise person should make special efforts for achieving factors which sustain the body,[2] for which the term "*Yoga Kṣemakara*" is used. The term "*yoga*" means the attainment of excellent strength as well as complexion and the term "*kṣema*" indicates the prevention of diseases, which could be possible by following the codes and conducts of *Sadavṛtta* (*Ācāra Rasāyana*) including *Rasāyana* Therapy.

Good health is something more than being free from diseases. The WHO has laid down that "Health is a state of complete physical, mental and social well being and not merely absence of disease on infirmity". Till recently it was difficult to find out the difinition of the word "Health" in any text book of modern medicine. The mechanismistic idea of disease left no room for the concept of health other than disease. Even this definition of WHO of positive health falls short of the definition of positive health as given in *Āyurveda*.

In this context it is important to go through the definition of healthy man as depicted by *Ācārya Śusruta*.[3]

---

१. सर्वमन्यत् परित्यज्य शरीरमनुपालयेत्।
तदभावे हि भावानां सर्वाभाव: शरीरिणाम्।।
(चरक निदान-६/७)

२. तस्मात् पुरुषो मति मानात्मन: शारीरेष्वेव योगक्षेमकरेषु प्रयतेत विशेषेण; शरीरं ह्यस्य मूलं, शरीरमूलश्च पुरुषो भवति।।
(चरक निदान ६/६)

३. समदोष: समाग्निश्च समधातु मलक्रिय:।
प्रसन्नात्मेन्द्रियमना: स्वस्थ इत्यभिधीयते।।
(सुश्रुत सूत्र-१५/४१)

According to this definition a healthy man is that who has—

1. Equilibrium of three *Doṣās* i.e. *Vāta, Pitta* and *Kapha*.

2. Normal status of *Koṣthāgni* (Digestion).

3. Normal status, equilibrium and condition of seven *Dhātūs* (tissue elements).

4. Besides, his *Ātma* (soul), *Indriās* (Sense Organs) and the *Manasa* (mind) should be happy and cheerful.

This definition of Health or *Swāsthya* covers the comprehensive well being of the total i.e. four dimensional life entity, the *Āyu*.[1] Thus it is evident that the concept of total health or *Swāsthya* as described in *Āyurveda* thousands of years back still has no parallel in any other discipline of medicine. It is the unique concept of total health or *Swāsthya* in *Āyurveda*.

Childhood and old age are the two extremes of life but none of the two have ever been liked by the mankind. One finds the real pleasure of life, if it is full of activities and vigour during the period of youthful age. One hates old age and dreads the death.

The *Rasāyana* Therapy of *Āyurveda* is one of the major methods of the preservation of health as described in *Āyurvedic* System of Medicine. The answer to prevent premature ageing also lies in *Rasāyana* Therapy. It may not be out of place to high light the current problems to which the *Rasāyana* Therapy may be the most rational answer.

---

१. शरीरेन्द्रिय सत्वात्मसंयोगो धारि जीवितम्।
नित्यगश्चानुबन्धश्च पर्य्यायैरायुरुच्यते।। (चरक सूत्र १/४२)

The present condition of human health around the globe is far from statisfactory. Whilst the developing countries are facing acute problems of physical health owing to undernutrition and infection, the affluent people of the west are living in an environment of anxiety and tension.

No doubt the modern medicine has practically solved the problems of infection through many a times resistant pathogenic organisms still stand as a challenge, and many metabolic and psychosomatic diseases e.g. Diabetes mellitus, Ischaemic Heart Disease, Hypertension, Peptic Ulcer, Hepatic Insufficiency, Thyrotoxicosis and Ulcerative Colitis etc. making the life miserable, look for other alternative measures for treatment and control. Similarly the toxicity and untoward effects of the currently used modern drugs are emerging as a major set back.

As an answer to sovle the problems of healthful longevity including mental development and resistance against diseases stands "*Rasāyana Tantra*", one of the clinical disciplines of *Aṣṭānga Āyurveda* (Eight fold *Āyurveda*). Different classics have defined *Rasāyana Tantra* in different words but with same central idea. *Ācārya Suśruta's* description in this respect is precise and scientific.

Ācārya Suśruta has defined *Rasāyana*[1] as the measure which prolongs longevity, develops positive health and mental faculties and imparts resistance and immunity against diseases. It appears to have been practised as an independent clinical discipline primarily as a positive health measure.

---

१. रसायन तन्त्रं नाम वयः स्थापनमायुर्मेधा बलकरं रोगापहरण समर्थं च। (सुश्रुत सूत्र-१/७)

With the passage of time this important branch of knowledge has ceased to be in practice in its appropriate form. Comprehensive efforts are needed to revive this useful discipline of *Āyurveda* for the welfare of the humanity at large.

In view of this fact a need was felt to bring out the total concept of *Rasāyana* Therapy by screening the entire *Āyurvedic* literature and the allied texts so that an uptodate idea may be framed about the original *Āyurvedic* concepts of *Rasāyana* Therapy for further scientific studies on these concepts.

Besides the uptodate development of the *Āyurvedic* concepts there is an equally urgent need of clinical evaluation of the real efficacy of the *Rasāyana* drugs and measures so that *Rasāyana* Therapy may be revived in its practical aspects at the earliest.

With this background the present book is presented for *Āyurvedic* scholars, teachers, students and physicians for having comprehensive and up to date knowledge of *Rasāyana Tantra* on scientific lines.

Chapter II

Historical Review of *Rasāyana* Therapy

Āyurveda is one of the most ancient systems of medicines in the world. Its origin can be traced back to the sacred *Vedās* which are considered the oldest scriptures on the human wisdom and civilisation. *Āyurveda* is the science of life which deals with good, bad, happy and unhappy life *(Āyu), its* promoters and non-promoters, measurement and nature.[1] "*Āyu*" means the conjunction of body, sense organs, mind and self and is known by the synonyms of "*Dhāri*, *Jīvitāma*, *Nītyaga* and *Anubandha*'.[2]

Rasāyana Therapy is one of the eight major clinical disciplines of *Aṣṭānga Āyurveda*. It appears to have been practised as an independent clinical discipline primarily as a positive health promoter medicine. A survey of the ancient literature traces the concept of *Rasāyana* Therapy as back as the *Vedic* ages. Though there is no systematic

---

१. हिताहितं सुखं दु:खमायुस्तस्य हिताहितम्।
मानं च तच्च यत्रोक्तमायुर्वेद: स उच्यते।।
(चरक सूत्र-१/४१)

२. शरीरेन्द्रिय सत्त्वात्मसंयोगो धारि जीवितम्।
नित्यगश्चानुबन्धश्च पर्यायैरायुरुच्यते।।
(चरक सूत्र-१/४२)

description of *Rasāyana Tantra* in *Vedās*, one finds the existence of similar thoughts in the *Vedic* literature. It is most unfortunate that this important branch '*Rasāyana Tantra*' of *Aṣṭānga Āyurveda* was on the verge of extinction. It is observed that *Rasāyana* Therapy is being practised as a part of *Kāyacikitsā* and not as an independent branch of *Āyurveda*. This has lead to the misconception that *Rasāyana* Therapy and *Kāyacikitsā* are clubbed together as one and the same branch of *Āyurveda*. But luckily recent trends in present times have shown that '*Rasāyana Tantra*' of *Āyurveda* is getting lot of recognition by *Āyurvedic* Scholars and this important branch of *Āyurveda* is being revived as "Geriatric Medicine." For the sake of convenience the description of '*Rasāyana Tantra*' can be studied under following heads indicating different periods (*kāla*)—

1. *Rasāyana* in *Vedic kāla*
2. *Rasāyana* in *Pauraṇika kāla*
3. *Rasāyana* in *Mahākāvya kāla*
4. *Rasāyana* in *Samhitā kāla*
5. *Rasāyana* in *Sangraha kāla*
6. *Rasāyana* in *Ādhunika kāla* (Modern Era)

It is important to note that the discriptions of *Rasāyana* as available in different texts of different periods is similar with the main emphasis on achieving longevity with healthy life.

Rasāyana in Vedic *Kāla*

Though there is no systematic description of *Rasāyana Tantra* in *Vedās*, one finds the existence of similar thoughts in the *Vedic* literature. In *Vedic* literature one finds definite evidences of the concept of rejuvenation and tissue regeneration. The *Vedās* have seriously considered the problem of ageing and its prevention. It has been the cherished wish of human race to achieve long life and to live at least for hundred years in perfect health. In *Atharva Veda* clear cut description is available about the desire of human beings to become '*Ajara*' and '*Amara*' i.e. to attain healthful longevity which is possible with the administration of *Rasāyana* Therapy.[1] In *Atharva veda* 8/7/4 a *Bheṣaja* "*Rohiṇī*" is described which has many properties including "*Jīvana Dāyaka*" property (which enhances life span).

Vedās are the basic and main source of knowledge for Indians and are considered as the oldest literature. The exact clear cut description of the word '*Rasāyana*' is not found in *Vedic* literature, but a number of *mantrās*, chantings and medicines have been described to attain long life. The description of divine *Rasāyana* agents like "*Soma Rasāyana*" is available in *Atharvaveda*. Common *Rasāyana* drugs like *Pippalī, Jivantī* and *Punarnavā* are described in *Vedās* describing clearly their superiority over other *Rasāyana* drugs.

Four types of treatment were prescribed in *Atharvaveda* for promotion of long life along with elimination of senility changes,[2] namely—

1. *Ātharvaṇī*
2. *Āngirasī*

---

१. देवस्य पश्य काव्यं न ममार न जीर्यति।
(अथर्ववेद-१०/८/३२)

२. आथर्वणी आंगिरसी दैवी मनुष्यजा उतः।
ओषधयः प्रजायन्ते यदा त्वं प्राणजिन्वसी।।
(अथर्ववेद-११/४/१६)

3. *Daivī*
4. *Manuṣyaja*

1. *Ātharvaṇi Cikitsā*

This treatment is done through a number of *mantrās* (holy hymns). It also includes "*Japa, Homa, Dāna* and *Swastivācana.*"

2. *Āngirasī Cikitsā*

This treatment is dependent over 'Mental Force' (*Mānsika Śakti*) of the individuals.

It has been described in various *Vedās* that a sort of '*Rasa*' is present in *Indriyās* and different parts of the body through which the life is maintained. Treatment done by using such *Rasās* is termed as '*Āngirasi Cikitsā*'.

3. *Daivi Cikitsā*

Treatment done with the help of natural resources like wind, water & earth etc. is known as "*Daivi Cikitsā*".

4. *Manuṣyaja Cikitsā*

It is the treatment done with the help of medicines prepared by human beings such as decoctions, powders, linctus, *bhasmās* and paste etc.

References are available in *Ṛgveda* that *Aśwani Kumārs* recommended *Rasāyana* Therapy to *Ṛṣi Kali* and his wife *Ghoṣā* and helped them to attain youthful age again.[1] *Aśwani Kumārs* were considered as *Vedic Vaidyās*.

---

१. युवं विप्रस्य जरणामुपेयुषः पुनः क्लेश्कृणुत युवद्वयः।
युवं वन्दनभृष्यदादुदवथुर्युवं सद्यो विष्पलामेतवे कृथः।।
(ऋग्वेद-१०/३९/८)

They were believed to be promoters of long life along with maintenance of health. *Aświni Kumārs* had converted so many emaciated and old persons into young, handsome and attractive individuals with the administration of *Rasāyana* Therapy. They were also called "*Daiva Bhiṣaka*" as *Devatās* (Gods) were also benefitted by them in achieving healthy long life.

In *Ṛgveda* 10/18/1-6 and *Atharvaveda* 2/13/4, 2/17/67, 3/11/1-4, 8/1/1-18, 8/2/1-11, 19/60/1-2, 19/67/1-8 specific descriptions resembling *Rasāyana* with the message of "*Jivema Śaradaha*; *Śatama*"[1] is available emphasising the healthful longevity.

A number of *auṣadhi* (medicines) having longevity effect promoting the health and life span (*Rasāyana Prabhāva*) are described in *Atharva Veda*. These include *Jivalā, Navāriṣā*, *Jīvanti*, *Trāyamāṇā*, *Sahamānā* and *Sahaswati*[2] etc. These medicines are described in *Atharva Veda* for the welfare of people. One can get rid of death by the use of these drugs. Several types of deaths are described in *Vedās*. At the same time protective measures from these deaths are also discussed.

In *Ṛgveda* 5/11/7, 9/113/4, *Atharvaveda* 16/2/2, 13/2/25, 7/52/8 and *Yajurveda* 40/17, 9/21, 3/1, 40/1 etc. Verses deal with the description of "*Sadavṛtta*" (Codes and Conducts of life) for achieving healthy longer life span. This description of "*Sadavṛtta*" resembles the description of "*Ācāra Rasāyana*" of *Ācārya Caraka*.

---

१. "जीवेम शरदः शतम्"

२. जीवलां नवारिषां जीवन्तीमोषधीमहम्।
त्रायमाणां सहमानां सहस्वतीमिह हुवेऽस्मा अरिष्टतातये।।
(अथर्ववेद-८/२/६)

In *Vedic* period death occuring after 100 years was called as "*Kāla Mṛtyu*" and that commensing before 100 years was termed as "*Akāla Mṛtyu.*" The attainment of *Dharma*, *Artha, Kāma* and *Mokṣa* is only possible when the person acquires healthy long life. Presently, *Āyurvedic* treatment which is aimed at the achievement of healthy long life is possible only with the administration of *Rasāyana* Therapy.

2. *Rasāyana* in *Paurāṇika Kāla*

Purāṇās are supposed to be old lectures delivered by *Ṛṣis* based on *Vedās*. At times *Purāṇa* is also accepted as the fifth *Veda*. In *Garura Purāṇa* therapeutics related description is available from chapter Nos. 146 to 200. These chapters contain vivid description of *Rasāyana Tantra*.

Agni Purāṇa contains description of "*Sidha Auṣadhāni*" (278) and "*Sarva Roga Haraṇi Auṣadhāni* (279). *Rasāyana* is essential for "*Dīrghāu*" (Longevity) and "*Brahmacarya*" (Celebacy). In "*Chandopniṣad*" 8/4.6 description regarding *Brahmacarya* and in "*Chandogya Upiniṣad*" 3/16 description regarding "*Dīrghāuṣya*" (Longevity) is available.

Reference is available in *Matsya Purāṇa* 3/6-8 that *Ācārya Kāśayapa* gained long life with the administration of *Rasāyana*. Following references also support the availability of *Rasāyana* related references in various *Purāṇās*—

* Long lifed *Sanata Kumara*, the son of Lord *Brahma* is supposed to be as *Urdhvarata* and *Yogadharma* (*Vāyu Purāṇa* 10/106, *Hari Vanṣa Purāṇa* 1/12, 17).

* *Uśava* and *Bhṛgu* had the knowledge of *Sanjīvana* (*Brahma Purāṇa* 3/32-72).

* There is descriptions of "*Mrita Sanjīvani*" in 285th Chapter of *Agni Purāṇa*. Similarly a number of preparations are described in 286th Chapter of *Agni Purāṇa*.

* Description is available in *Bhāgwata Purāṇa* about the methods of making a man young (regaining the youthfulness), king *Śāntanu* used this skill for making older persons look like young ones.

3. *Rasāyana* in *Mahākāvya Kāla*

* Various holy *mantrās* are described in *Bhāgwata Gītā* and *Rāmāyaṇa* for obtaining offsprings and longevity which have close resemblance with *Rasāyana* and *Vājikarṇa* as described in *Āyurveda*.

* *Brahma Samhitā* created by Lord *Brahmā* ji contains various preparations and two preparations of *Brahma Rasāyana*, latter described by *Ācārya Caraka*.

* "*Cikitsā Sāra*" and "*Nāḍi Parīkṣā*" are the two books supposed to be written by *Aśwani Kumārs*. These contain description of *Cyavanaprāśa*.

* Lord *Indra* created "*Balabhita Samhitā*" which contains descriptions of *Ācāra Rasāyana* and many single *Rasāyana* drugs.

* *Rasāyana* in *Rāmāyaṇa*

There are a number of examples of description of *Rasāyana* which are used to rejuvenate the body.

1. *Vaidya Suśen* has described "*Mrita-Sanjivani*," a drug in reference to long life.

2. *Agastya Ṛṣi* is a known person who lived long (*Vālmiki Ramāyaṇa Aranyakānda* 11/82)

3. Brother of *Agastya Ṛṣi* is called as *Mṛtyunjaya* (*Vālmiki Rāmāyaṇa Aranyakānd* 11/55)

4. *Lopamudra,* wife of *Agastya Ṛṣi* is also supposed to have lived long (*Vālmiki Ramāyaṇa Araṇyakānda*)

*** *Rasāyana* in *Mahābhārata***

A number of examples are available in *Mahābhārata* to show presence of references of *Rasāyana* in it—

1. The son of Lord *Brahmā*, *Sanata Kumār* had ever youthfulness (*Śāntiparva*)

2. Revitalisation of Demons killed by *Uśava* in battle field.

3. Loss of old age of *Cyavana Ṛṣi*. (*Mahā Śānti* 35/24)

4. *Rasāyana* in *Samhitā Kāla*

Āyurveda is immortal and its main sources are *Vedās* which are *Anādi* and *Apouruṣya* (i.e. not written by human beings). *Āyurveda* has divine origin. *Āyurveda* is accepted as *Upaveda* of *Atharvaveda*.

Though the word '*Rasāyana Tantra*' is used, no separate *Samhitā* or Book is available by this name. The *Roga Nirodhaka Śakti* i.e. body resistance or body immunity towards diseases or the power to oppose the disease process and preventive medicine also are covered under *Rasāyana*. A number of *Samhitās* written by *Ācārya Agnīveṣa, Bhela, Jatukarṇa, Pārāśara* etc. are not available in present times. Not only the *Samhitās* but other books related to *Samhitā Kāla* have also described the utility of *Rasāyana* both theoretically and practically. Detailed description of *Rasāyana Tantra* is available in *Bṛhata Trayī*, *Laghu Trayī* and other books belonging to this period.

Rasāyana in *Caraka Samhitā* (2000 B.C.)

In *Caraka Uttarārdha* the first Chapter of *Cikitsā Sthāna* is devoted to *Rasāyana*. It proves that *Ācārya Caraka* has given great importance to *Rasāyana Tantra*. The first Chapter on '*Rasāyana Adhikāra*' has four subchapters (*Pāda*). Various principles of *Rasāyana* Therapy have been established. The concept of administration of *Rasāyana* Therapy in the form of "*Vātātapika* and *Kutī Prāveṣika*" has been put forward by *Caraka* for the first time. Definition of *Rasāyana*, its utility and various *Rasāyana yoga* (compound *Rasāyana* preparations) are described in details. There is specific mention of "*Cayavanaprāśa*" a *Rasāyana* which was administered to "*Ṛṣi Cayavana*" who had gone very weak due to emaciation of various *Dhātūs* and had attained old oge. With the administration of "*Cayavanaprāṣa*" to him, *Maharṣi Cayavana* regained his lost youthfulness.[1]

Ācārya Caraka has described various *Rasāyana yoga* in *Caraka Samhitā* viz. *Caraka cikitsā* 1/1 contains 6 *yoga*, 1/2 contains 37 *yoga*, 1/3 contains 16 *yoga* and 1/4 contains 4 *Rasāyana yoga*. It shows that *Rasāyana* Therapy was at its peak in the period of *Ācārya Caraka*. *Ācāra Rasāyana* has been described in details.

Rasāyana in *Śusruta Samhitā* (2000 B.C.)

It appears that *Rasāyana Cikitsā* has been given less

---

१. प्राणकामाः पुरा जीर्णाश्च्यवनाद्या महर्षयः।
रसायनैः शिवरेतैर्बभूवुरमितायुषः।।
(च.चि. १/२/२०)

emphasis by *Suśruta* in comparison to *Caraka*. This is probably due to the fact that *Suśruta* is mainly surgery oriented while *Caraka* is predominantly medicine oriented.

Suśruta has described *Rasāyana* as an agent which is capable of maintaining longevity, intellect, vigour, vitality and which can prevent diseases[1]. *Suśruta* has described *Rasāyana* in four chapters, 27-30 in *Cikitsā Sthāna*. Out of these four, two chapters deal with "*Divya Rasāyana*" whose existence is doubtful today. *Suśruta* has advocated the use of *Rasāyana* Therapy in youthful age. He has given comprehensive, systematic and scientific classification of *Rasāyana* Therapy. The concept of "*Naimittika Rasāyana*" is the original contribution of *Ācārya Suśruta*. New *Rasāyana Dravyās* and *yogās* have been added by *Suśruta*.

Rasāyana in *Vāgabhatta Samhita* (600 A.D.)

Chapter No. 49th of *Aṣṭānga Sangraha* and 39th of *Aṣṭānga Hṛdya* deal with *Rasāyana Tantra*. The description of *Vāgabhatta* about *Rasāyana Tantra* has very close resemblance with the description of *Caraka*. Definition, uses, types, modes of administration, age of administration and list of various *Rasāyana yogās* has been described in details. *Vāgabhatta* has emphasized the administration of *Rasāyana* Therapy in young and middle age. Several new single *Rasāyana* drugs and *Rasāyana Yoga* have been added, like *Rasona*, Plāndu etc.

---

१. रसायनतन्त्रं नाम वयः स्थापनमायुर्मेधाबलकरं रोगापहरणसमर्थं च।
(सु.सू. १/७)

5. *Rasāyana* in *Sangraha Kāla* (8 A.D. to 16 A.D.)

Sangraha Kāla is also known as *Madhya Kāla or Tīkā Kāla*. During this period the number of independent *Samhitā*s produced was reduced, but a number of *Samhitā*s were written by compiling the old *Samhitā*s e.g. *Śārangadhara* (13th century), *Bhāvaprakāṣa* (16th century) etc. In these *Samhitā*s the authors updated the information on the subject and discussed it in more details. Along with it a number of new drugs were incorporated keeping in view of *Doṣa*, *Kāla* and other conditions etc. Actually the art of compiling started after the period of *Ācārya Vāgabhatta*. *Rasāyana* Therapy became more famous during this period.

In *Śārangadhara Samhitā Rasāyana* and *Vājikaraṇa* are described in 4th chapter of *Pūrva Khanda*.

In *Bhela Samhitā* the use of *Triphalā Rasāyana* is described.

In *Kāśyapa Samhitā* the description of *Rasāyana* and *Vājikaraṇa* is available in *Kalpa Sthāna*.

In "*Cikitsā Kalikā*" written by *Tistācārya Rasāyana* and *Vājikaraṇa* are described from *Sūtra* 300 to 399. *Rasa Śastra* was in lime light during this period. As a result along with herbal drugs, a number of *Rasauṣdhi* made of *Rasa* (Mercury) and *Gandhaka* (Sulphur) also came into wide usage. *Cakrapāṇī* has described *Tāmra Rasāyana* consisting of *Pārada*, *Gandhaka*, *Tāmra* and *Abhraka*. *Cakrapāṇi Dutta* has incorporated a number of *Rasāyana Yogās* made of *Rasauṣadhi* in his book '*Cakradutta*'.

In *Rasendra Cūṛamaṇi Kānta Rasāyana*, *Vanga Rasāyana, Sīsa Rasāyana* and *Pittala Rasāyana* are described.

In *Banga Sen Śivā Gutikā, Tāmra Rasāyana, Gandhaka Rasāyana* and *Guggulu Rasāyana* are described.

In *Bhaiṣjaya Ratnāwali Rasāyana* and *Vājikaraṇa* are described separately.

In *Rasa Ratnakara Rasāyana* and *Vājikaraṇa* are described in *Rasāyana Khanda*.

In *Rasa Pradīpa* and *Bṛhata Rasa Pradīpa Mṛtunjaya Rasa, Trailokya Mohana Rasa* and *Loha Rasāyana* are mentioned.

6. *Rasāyana* in *Ādhunika Kāla*

Today people lead their lives in a more sophisticated way. Improper food habits, altered life styles, persistent stress, water and air pollution etc. and so many other factors are executing serious dangerous affects on human life. To prevent and get rid of these harmful effects, people are to be administered *Rasāyana* Therapy for improving their body resistance.

According to principles of *Āyurveda*, the health of a healthy individual is to be maintained and protected through a number of measures like *Dinacaryā*, *Rātri Caryā*, and *Ṛtu Caryā* etc. *Rasāyana* Therapy plays an important role in maintaining and promoting positive health of individuals by promoting their body resistance i.e. "Immunity" against diseases. Now a days more emphasis is laid down over prevention of diseases rather than curing them after they have appeared in the body. It is a well known saying that prevention is better than the cure. This objective could easily be achieved with the help of *Rasāyana* Therapy.

Various *Āyurvedic* Scholars are engaged in research activities in the field of *Rasāyana* on various scientific parameters. It has been proved scientifically that various "*Medhya Rasāyana*" drugs have potent Psychotropic effects. They can be used effectively in the management of various stress induced disorders. *Medhya Rasāyana* drugs possess potent anti-anxiety effects. On administration in human body they produce tranquility of mind without producing hang over effects. Similarly "*Naimittika Rasāyana*" drugs are used with great success in specific inhibition of a particualr disease besides obtaining '*Rasāyana Prabhāva*' in the body. It has been proved by various scientists that *Rasāyana* Drugs have specific "Anti-Aging" properties due to their anti-oxidant effects.

Efforts have been made to compile the scattered material of '*Rasāyana Tantra*' in various *Āyurvedic Samhitās* systematically, in a new form, having scientific basis. Latest concepts of Geriatric Medicine have also been incorporated at appropriate palces to make this book more informative.

Chapter III

Rasāyana Tantra

Etymology of *Rasāyana*

The term "*Rasāyana*" used in *Āyurveda*, denotes a specific meaning. It consists of two words viz.—

(i) *Rasa*

(ii) *Ayana*

A. Rasa

According to *Pāṅinī* grammer the word *Rasa* is derived from the root "*Rasa-Rasatiti Rasaha*", meaning that which moves. *Suśruta* has also emphasized that the term "*Rasa*" denotes that thing which moves day and night.[1]

In classical *Sanskrit* literature many interpretations have been made of the word *Rasa* as discussed here under—

1. **In *Kāvya Śāstra***—In *Kāvya* (Poetry) the term '*Rasa*' is used to express "*Vibhāva, Anubhāva* and *Sancāri Bhāva*" e.g. *Vīra Rasa, Karuṇā Rasa* etc.[2]

---

१. तत्र 'रस' गतौ धातु: अहरहर्गच्छतीत्यतो रस:। (सुश्रुत सूत्र १४/१३)

२. रस्यते आस्वाद्यते विभानुभावसंचरिभि: संयुक्तत्वेन इति रस रूपेण परिणत: इत्यादि स्थायी भाव: सोऽयं रस: काव्यात्मभूत:शृङ्गारादि साहित्य विषय:।

2. **In *Rasa Śāstra*—**The term '*Rasa*' denotes mercury in *Rasa Śāstra*[1]

3. **In Philosophical Aspects—**The '*Yogi Puruṣa*' and 'Holy People' worship to God, meditate and concentrate in order to attain '*Mokṣa*'. During these processes, the satisfaction and inner joy felt by these people is also referred to '*Rasa*'. The super divine power, the almighty "*Brahma*" is denoted by the term '*Rasa*'.[2]

4. **In *Dravya Guṇa*—**In the field of *Dravyaguṇa Śāstra* (Materia Medica) '*Rasa*' denotes that which is perceptible to Tongue.[3]

5. **In *Śarīra Kriyā* (Physiology)—**According to physiology of *Āyurveda*, *Rasa* denotes the end products of the digestion of food. After consuming the food and drinks, the food having been metabolised by digestive ferments (*Agni*) of the living body, the residue which is excreted and its essence absorbed in the system is known as '*Rasa*'.[4]

---

१. रसनात सर्वधातुनां रस्यते वा रसोमत:।

(रस रत्न समुच्चय-१/७)

२. रस्यते आस्वाद्यते सान्द्रानन्दनिर्भरत्वेन आध्यात्मचित्तमयै:। योगिभिरिति: यदा रसति सर्वदा अनपायित्वेन स्थितो भवति इति रस: ब्रह्म।।

३. रसो निपाते द्रव्याणां, विपाक: कर्मनिष्ठया।
वीर्य यावदधीवासान्निपाताच्चोपलभ्यते।।

(चरक सूत्र २६/६६)।

४. तत्र पाञ्चभौतिकस्य चतुर्विधस्य षडरसस्य द्विविधवीर्यस्याष्ट विधवीर्यस्य वाऽनेकगुणस्योपयुक्तस्याहारस्य सम्यक् परिणतस्य यस्तेजोभूत: सार: परमसूक्ष्म: स 'रस' इत्युच्यते। (सुश्रुत सूत्र १४/३)

6. **In *Śarīra Racnā* (Anatomy)**—According to anatomy of *Āyurveda*, '*Rasa*' denotes the first element of tissue building (*Dhāthurūpa Rasa*) which is the only source of nourishment to all the tissues of the body. This goes on circulating day and night without interruption, supplying nutrition to all living cells of the body.[1]

7. **In *Bhaiṣjaya Kalpanā***—In *Bhaiṣjaya Kalpanā* the term "*Swarasa*" represents "*Rasa*" which is obtained by squeezing various *dravyās* (Drugs).[2]

In the present context of *Rasāyana*, the word '*Rasa*' has the sense of end products of digestion. It has been mentioned that the food which is usually composed of five fundamental material principles, being classified under four different heads (as drinks, edibles etc.) has six different tastes or it consists of two properties viz. *Śita* (Cool) and *Uṣṇa* (Hot) or eight fold potencies and of a variety of other efficacious virtues, is fully digested with the help of the *Jātharāgni* (Biofire) giving rise to *Rasa* (Lymph, Chyle) which is extremely thin in its consistency and which forms the essence of the assimilated food.

According to modern physiology, the end products of protein and carbohydrate digestion are absorbed by the vascular capillaries in the villi and are drained into the portal system (chyme). Fats mainly pass through the lacteals of villi and are carried by the lymphatics (chyle). The large intestine mainly absorbs water, saline, glucose and alcohol. Certain other drug substances may be

---

१. तस्य हृदयं स्थानं, स हृदयाच्चतुर्विंशति धमनीरनुप्रविश्योर्ध्वगा दश दशाधोगामिन्यश्चतस्त्रश्च तिर्यग्गा: कृत्स्नं शरीर महरहस्तर्पयति वर्द्धयति धारयति यापयति चादृष्टहेतुकेन कर्मणा। (सुश्रुत सूत्र १४/३)

२. यन्त्रनिष्पीड़िताद् द्रव्याद्रस: स्वरस उच्यते।

absorbed which is the essence of total food digested by an individual.

This '*Rasa*' is the only source of nourishment to all the tissues of the body. This goes on circulating day and night without interruption, supplying nutrition to all living cells of the body. Further it is mentioned that the essence of food provides nutrition to *Rasa Dhātu Rupa Rasa* (Plasma and such other fluid contents of the body), *Rakta* (blood constituents), *Māmsa* (muscels), *Meda* (fat), *Asthi* (bones), *Majjā* (marrow), *Śukra* (semen constituent), *Oja* (essence of all *Dhātūs*), the material constituents of the five sense organs (which are the essence of the tissue elements), joints, ligaments and mucin etc. of the body.

Hence the specific meaning of '*Rasa*' in context with *Rasāyana* is the essence of food i.e. *Āhāra Rasa*.

Rasāyana Therapy is defined as the means by which one gets the excellence of *Rasa*, *Rakta* etc. (tissue elements). This *Āhāra Rasa* (essence of food) is known to be the premier nutrition of the body tissue, hence it is counted as a precursor of all tissues. *Āhāra Rasa* is free from all sorts of impurities and permeates the minutest vessels and capillaries.

The production of the best quality of *Rasa* in the system is therefore the first and foremost duty of a physician in order to maintain the health of an individual. In other words quantitative and qualitative normalcy of *Rasa* is normalcy of health. The possibility of induced regeneration of different cells, tissues, and organs, the prevention of the process of aging and disease could well be conceived by the production of a good quality of *Rasa* in the living body.

The other characteristic of *Rasa* is its mobile nature. This uninterrupted mobility is also essential for life, because impairment of the circulation of this body fluid results in diseases and decay. So it is important to note that this body fluid of good quality should not only present in adequate quantity, but also it should be able to permeate (circulate) through out various cells of the body to provide the type of nourishment they need, so as to physical fitness of the organs of a living body takes place. The activity of *Rasāyana* Therapy is concentrated in this proper *Rasa's* formation level, where it is mostly required for the qualitative and quantitative standard production of the end products of digestion.

B. *Ayana*

The other word constituting the term '*Rasāyana*' is '*Ayana*.' According to *Sanskrit* grammar the word '*Ayana*' is made from इण धातु, ''इण गतौ धातु'' which has different meanings–

(i) *Jñāna* (knowledge)

(ii) *Gamana* (Way, Progression)

(iii) *Prāpti* (Attainment).

The word '*Ayana*' is quite familiar to *Sanskrit* literature i.e. *Rāmāyaṇa*, *Nārāyaṇa*, *Uttarāyaṇa* and *Dakṣiṇāyaṇa* etc. From above connotation *Rāmāyaṇa* means,

(i) Which acquaints about the supreme reality, the '*Rāma*.'

(ii) The way to supreme reality, the '*Rāma*.'

(iii) The process which attains to the '*Rāma*'. *Nārāyaṇa* is also used in same context. But *Uttarāyaṇa* and *Dakṣiṇāyaṇa* represent only second connotation i.e. the sun's progress towards north of the equator or towards south of the equator.

But in the present context of *Rāsāyana*, the word '*Ayana*' has the sense of attainment. Thus the term '*Rasāyana*' is a compound word which denotes the process/ways/means of attaining standard *Āhāra Rasa* of good quality for the body. How to achieve the goal of the desired *Rasa* in the body and how to help the body to attain perfect health and ability by such a method is the main theme (scope) of this particular clinical branch of *Āyurveda*.[1]

Thus from the point of view of grammar the word '*Rasāyana*' means the ways of obtaining good quality of '*Rasa*'.[2-3]

Nirukti of *Rasāyana*

To understand the exact meaning of a word, it is important to understand its literary meaning which is possible only with the "*Nirukti*," of that word. Following meanings of the word '*Rasāyana*' are derived from the point of view of its *Nirukti*—

1. '*Rasa*' refers to its place of availability in reference to *Rasa-Raktādi Dhātūs*.[4]

---

१. लाभोपायो हि शस्तानाम् रसादिनां रसायनम्
(चरक चिकित्सा-१/१/८)

२. अयन-आसमन्तात्-पूर्णतः-अयनं = आयनम्।
रसस्य आयनं = रसायनम्।

३. रसस्य अयनं "लाभोपायो" रसायनम्।।

४. रसस्य अयनमिव। रसस्य अयनमिति।

2. The means of attaining *Rasa-Raktādi Dhātūs* are termed as *Rasāyana*.[1]

3. *Rasāyana* is that which has milk (*Dugdha*) as its root cause. Here *Dugdha* (milk) is treated to be *Rasāyana*.[2]

4. *Rasāyana* is that which attributes *Rasa-Taila* like *snigdha* (lubricant) properties.[3]

Synonyms of *Rasāyana*

After screening the *Āyurvedic* literature in the form of various *Samhitās*, it is observed that no clear cut and specific synonyms are described of *Rasāyana*. But depending upon their therapeutic effects and properties, following synonyms of *Rasāyana* can be developed—

1. *Jarā Vyādhi Nāśaka*

2. *Jarā Vyādhi Vidhwansī*

Since *Rasāyana* agents destroy the *Jarā* (Premature Aging) and *Vyādhi* (*Roga*-Diseases), hence they can be termed as *Jarā Vyādhi Nāśaka* or *Jarā Vyādhi Vidhwansī*.

3. *Jarā Vyādhi Utpatti Pratibandhaka*

Rasāyana agents prevent the occurrence of *Jara* and *Vyādhi* hence they may be termed as *Jarā-Vyādhi Utaptti Pratibandhaka*.

4. *Sarvopaghātaśamnīya*

Rasāyana can pacify almost all the grievances (Disorders), hence they may be termed as *Sarvopaghātaśamnīya*.

---

१. रसा: रसरक्तादय: ईयन्ते प्राप्यन्ते अनेन इति।

२. रसो दुग्धं अयनं मूल यस्य तत् रसायनम्।

३. रसायन् तैलादीन् अयते प्राप्नोति अनेन इति।

5. *Vaya Sthāpana*

Rasāyana prevents and destroys several disorders and in turn may lead to longevity by preventing premature aging, hence it is logical to call *Rasāyana* with the synonymous word *Vayasthāpana*.

Definition of *Rasāyana*

* Literally the word *Rasāyana* refers as the means of obtaining optimum standard of *Rasa Dhātu*.[1]

Different classics of *Āyurveda* have defined *Rasāyana* in different words but with the same central theme.

* *Ācārya Caraka* has described *Rasāyana* as the means of obtaining the best qualities of *Rasādi Dhātūs*,[2] (tissue elements). Various tissues of body get nourishment from *Āhāra Rasa*, so best quality of *Rasa* leads to the formation of best qualities of other *Dhātūs*. Thus *Rasāyana* is that process by which all the body tissues are nourished. Consequently *Rasāyana* helps in regeneration, revival and revitalisation of all body tissues/*Dhātūs*.

* On the comments of *Ācārya Caraka's* definition, *Ācārya Gangādhara* has mentioned *Rasāyana* as a particular measure by which one can gain longevity, lasting memory, vigour and vitality etc.[3]

---

१. (i) अयनं आसमन्तात पूर्णतः अयनं त्र आयनं रसस्य आयनं रसायनम्।
(ii) रसस्य आयनं लाभोपायो रसानयम्।।

२. लाभोपायो हि शस्तानाम् रसादीनां रसायनम्।

(चरक चिकित्सा-१/१/८)

३. दीर्घमायुः स्मृतिं मेधामारोग्यं तरुणं वयः।
प्रभावर्ण स्वरौदार्यं देहेन्द्रियबलं परम्।।

(चरक चिकित्सा-१/१/७ गंगाधर)

In *Caraka Samhitā* it has also been mentioned that *Rasāyana Dravyās* are usually alleviative of diseases, virilific and promotive of vigour in healthy individuals.

* *Ācārya Suśruta* has defined *Rasāyana*[1] as the measure which deals with the problems of youthful age, prolongs longevity, develops positive health and mental faculties and imparts resistance and immunity against diseases.

Ācārya Dalhaṇa, the commentator of *Suśruta Samhitā* has expressed his views explaining the word "*Vaya-Sthāpana*" which has got two meanings[2]—

(i) Which maintains the age of hundred years or more.

(ii) Which helps in alleviating the senility and maintaing young age for a longer period.

Ācārya Dalhaṇa further adds that the natural tendency to hunger, thirst, old age, death, sleep etc. are inhibited by the use of *Rasāyana*.[3]

It has been mentioned that *Rasāyana Dravyās* perform the action through *Rasa*, *Guṅa,* *Vīrya,* *Vipāka* and

---

१. रसायनतन्त्रं नाम वयःस्थापनमायुर्मेधाबलकरं रोगापहरण समर्थं च।
(सुश्रुत सूत्र-१/७)

२. वयः स्थापनं वर्षशतायुः स्थापनं आयुष्कालं शताधिकमपि करोति।
अन्ये तु वयःस्थापनं जरापहरणं तारुण्यं बहुकाल स्थापयतीत्यर्थः।।
(सुश्रुत सूत्र-१/८-डल्हण)

३. यद्यपि स्वभावो निष्प्रत्यनिकः तथापि रसायन प्रभावात...।
.... स्वभाव व्याधि प्रतिसिध्यते।।
(सुश्रुत चिकित्सा-२९/१-डल्हण)

Prabhāva on the seven *Dhātūs* and produce longevity, strength, vigour and lasting young age in the subjects.[1]

* *Ācārya Śārangadhara* has defined *Rasāyana* to be an agent which prevents ageing and diseases.[2] It is important to understand that the term aging denotes "premature aging."

* In *Tattwa Candrikā*, it has been mentioned that *Rasāyana* is the method which produces special *Rasa* in the body which not only destroys the old age; but also prevents the old age.

* Different scholars *Sudānta Sen, Yogendra Nāth Sen, Aruṅ Dutta, Bhāva Miṣra* and *Yoga Ratnākara* etc. have defined *Rasāyana* in similar way and they appear to be greatly influenced by *Ācārya Caraka*. They all define *Rasāyana* as a measure which may cure or prevent the diseases and aging.

* In *Bhaiṣajya Ratnāwali, Bhāva Prakāśa* and *Cakradutta Rasāyana* is defined to be that measure which prevents the aging and diseases.[3]

The word *Rasa* also represents the seven *Dhātūs* because they are all nourished by *Rasa* or yield of *Rasa*. State of this *Rasa* in the body directly governs the state of health of an individual. So the means of obtaining optimum standard of *Rasa* is known to be *Rasāyana*.

---

१. रसादि धातुनामयनमाप्ययनम्.........रसायनम्।

(सुश्रुत चिकित्सा-२७/१-डल्हण)

२. रसायनं च तज्ज्ञेयं यज्जराव्याधिनाशनम्।

(शारङ्गधर संहिता पूर्वखण्ड-४/१३)

३. यज्जराव्याधि विध्वंसि......................... भेषजं तद्रसायनम्।

(भा० प्र० ७३/१)

Thus the *Rasāyana* is a specialised type of treatment influencing the fundamental aspects of the organism viz. *Agni*, and the *Srotāmsi*, leading to an over all improvement in the organism which affords prevention of aging, resistance against diseases, bodily strength and improvement in mental faculties.

Rasāyana kā Prayojana and *Phala*

Contributions of *Rasāyana* Therapy

As already stated that *Āyurveda* has two objectives[1]—

(i) To maintain the health of healthy individuals.

(ii) To cure the diseases of diseased ones.

For accomplishing these objectives of *Āyurveda*, two types of medicines are described[2]—

(i) *Swathasyorjaskara*

(ii) *Roganuta* or *Rogaghna*

The definition of *Caraka* regarding *Rasāyana* reveals the fact that *Rasāyana* drugs possess both these activities because a drug which is *Swasthasyorjaskara* will efficiently prevent the occurrence of diseases in subjects. *Śārangadhara* has clearly indicated that *Rasāyana* drugs prevent aging and diseases.[3] *Ācārya Suśruta* has supported this concept and he has very clearly stated that *Rasāyana* drugs are *Urjaskara* in nature, that is why these drugs prevent diseases and old age.[4]

---

१. इह खल्वायुर्वेद प्रयोजनं व्याध्युपसृष्टानां
व्याधि परिमोक्षः, स्वस्थस्य स्वास्थ्य रक्षणं च।।
(सुश्रुत सूत्र-१/१४)

२. चरक चिकित्सा-१/१/४

३. शारंगधर संहिता पूर्वखण्ड-४/१३.

४. सुश्रुत सूत्र-१/७.

While describing the properties of *Rasāyana*, *Ācārya Caraka* has mentioned that on administration of *Rasāyana*, one attains longevity, memory, intelligence, freedom from disorders, youthful age, excellence of lusture, complexion and voice, optimum strength of physique and sense organs, successful words, respectability and brilliance. *Rasāyana* (promotive treatment) means the way for attaining excellent *Rasa Dhātu* etc.[1]

In *Aṣṭānga Sangraha* and *Aṣṭānga Hṛdya* similar properties of *Rasāyana* are mentioned. *Rasāyana* has so many positive effects over the body of individuals that it is compared to be similar to *Amṛta* (Nectar) in qualities.

Appreciating the efficacy of *Rasāyana* Therapy, *Caraka* has mentioned that if it is administrated as per the directions and norms laid down for the purpose, one may acquire '*Brahma*' or may attain '*Mokṣha*'.[2] References are available in *Caraka Samhitā* that *Ṛṣis* used to take *Rasāyana* methodically and regularly. As a result they could beat old age, weakness, emaciation, diseased states and death and used to enjoy age of thousands of years.[3]

---

१. दीर्घमायुः स्मृतिं मेधामारोग्यं तरुणं वयः।
प्रभावर्णस्वरौदार्यं देहेन्द्रियबलं परम्।।
वाक्सिद्धिं प्रणतिं कान्तिं लभते ना रसायनात्।
लाभोपायो हि शस्तानां रसादीनां रसायनम्।।

(चरक चिकित्सा-१/१/७-८)

२. न केवलं दीर्घमिहायुरश्नुते रसायनं यो विधिवन्निषेवते।
गतिं स देवर्षिनिषेवितां शुभां प्रपद्यते ब्रह्म तथेति चाक्षयम्।।

(चरक चिकित्सा-१/१/८०)

३. न जरां न च दौर्बल्यं नातुर्यं निधनं न च।
जग्मुर्वर्षसहस्राणि रसायनपराः पुरा।।

(चरक चिकित्सा-१/१/७९)

It has been stated that as *Devtās* (Gods) used to drink *Amṛta* (Nectar), Snakes used to take *Sudhā*, similarly in olden times *Ṛṣis* used to take *Rasāyana* Therapy regularly.[1]

In *Suśruta Samhitā* several types of *Medhāyuṣkāmīya Rasāyana* are described, which if used regularly, a man who is on death bed, can be saved. The king could be brought under one's control provided he takes *Rasāyana* Therapy regularly.[2]

In reference to *Ācāra Rasāyana*, it is mentioned that by properly following the codes and conducts of life style and *Sadavṛtta* one attains improved mental faculties leading to involvement in such activities which lead to longevity.[3]

Science of Rejuvenation has for its specific object the prolongation of human life and the invigoration of memory and the vital organs of man. It deals with recepies which enable a man to retain his manhood or

---

१. यथाऽमराणाममृतं यथा भोगवतां सुधा।
तथाऽभवन्महर्षिणां रसायनविधिः पुरा।।
(चरक चिकित्सा-१/१/७८)

२. प्राश्यारिष्टगृहीतोऽपि मुच्यते प्राणसंशयात्।
शतावरीघृतं सम्यगुपयुक्तं दिने दिने।
सक्षौद्रं ससुवर्णं च नरेन्द्र स्थापयेद्वशे।।
(सुश्रुत चिकित्सा-२८/२०-२१)

३. सतताध्ययनं वादः परतन्त्रावलोकनम्।
तद्विद्याचार्यसेवा च बुद्धि मेधाकरो गुणः।
आयुष्यं भोजनं जीर्णं वेगानां चाविधारणम्
ब्रह्मचर्यमहिंसा च साहसानां च वर्जनम्।।
(सुश्रुत चिकित्सा-२८/२७-२८)

youthful vigour upto good old age and which generally serves to make the human systems invulnerable to disease and decay.

Rejuvenation Therapy has unimaginable and wonderful effects. It promotes life, maintains positive health, preserves youth and cures morbid sleep, drowsiness, physical as well as mental fatigue, laziness and weakness. It maintains proper balance amongst *Vāta, Pitta* and *Kapha*. It produces stability; cures slothness of muscles, stimulates digestion and metabolism and brings about excellence in lusture, complexion as well as voice. By the administration of *Rasāyana* Therapy, the great sages like *Cayavana* etc. regained their youth and were liked most by women. Their muscles became compact and stable. They were indowed with excellence of strength, complexion and senses. They were persons of unchallangeable prowess every where. They developed powers of resistance of hardships.[1]

In older age *Maharṣi Cayavana* etc. succeeded in attaining long life by using these auspicious *Rasāyana* recipies. They were able to pursue their religious studies, *Tapa* (Penance), *Brahamacarya* (Celibacy), spiritual knowledge and meditation as much as they desired and also attained heaven. Therefore persons desirous of attaining long life, vitality and happiness should practice Rejuvenation Therapy with complete devotion according to the prescribed procedures.[2]

---

१. प्राणकामाः शुश्रूषध्वमिदमुच्यमानममृत ....।
.... सर्वत्राप्रतिहत पराक्रमाः क्लेशसहाश्च।।
(चरक चिकित्सा-१/२/३)

२. प्राणकामाः पुरा जीर्णाश्च्यवनाद्या महर्षयः।
... ...
... ...
रसायनविधिः सेव्यो विधिवत्सुसमाहितैः।।
(चरक चिकित्सा-१/२/२०-२२)

From the above it seems that such excellent results of the Rejuvenation (*Rasāyana*) Therapy will be found when one should use these recipies according to the prescribed procedures in persons who are devoid of vulgar habits, who are not engaged in multifarious types of work and who are having self control.[1]

Classification of *Rasāyana*

Ācārya Suśruta has contributed a comprehensive classification of *Rasāyana*. Commentator *Dalhaṅa* has improved it further. In *Caraka Samhitā* no such complete classification of *Rasāyana* is available. But in *Caraka Samhitā* methods of *Rasāyana* Therapy are described in details.

According to the contents, usage and scope of various measures *Rasāyana* may be classified as follows—The following classification emphasises the mode of administration, mode of actions and purpose of administration of *Rasāyana*—

1. According to Mode of Administration of *Rasāyana*[2]

(i) *Kutiprāveśika* (In door Regimen)

(ii) *Vātātapika* (Out door Regimen)

(iii) *Droṅī Prāveśika* (Special Regimen)

---

१. स्थिता महर्षय: पूर्वं नहि किञ्चिद्रसायनम्।
ग्राम्यानामन्यकार्याणां सिध्यत्यप्रयतात्मनाम्।।

(चरक चिकित्सा-१/३/८)

२. रसायनानां द्विविधं प्रयोगमृषयो विदु:।
कुटीप्रावेशिकं चैव वातातपिकमेव च।।

(चरक चिकित्सा-१/१/१६)

2. According to Purpose of Administration

(a) *Kāmya Rasāyana*[1] (Promotor of normal health)

(i) *Prāṅa Kāmya* (Promotor of life-vitality and longevity)

(ii) *Medhā Kāmya* (Promotor of intellect)

(iii) *Sri Kāmya* (Promotor of Complexion and Lusture)

(b) *Naimittika Rasāyana* (Promotors of specific vitality in specific diseases)

(c) *Ājasrika Rasāyana* (Dietary *Rasāyana*)[2]

3. According to Mode of Action[3]

(i) *Samśodhana Rasāyana*

(ii) *Samśamana Rasāyana*

4. Ācāra *Rasāyana*[4] (Conduct *Rasāyana*)

It is of three types—

(i) *Āhāra Rasāyana* (Dietary Modalities)

(ii) *Ācāra Rasāyana* (Behavioural Modalities)

(iii) *Dravya Rasāyana* (Drug based measures)

5. According to *Bheṣja Bheda* (According to Drug Measures Used)

(i) *Dravya Bhūta Rasāyana* (Drug *Rasāyana*)

---

१. पुनश्च त्रिविधं काम्यं, नैमित्तिकम्, आजस्त्रिक च।
(सुश्रुत चिकित्सा-२७/१-डल्हण)

२. आजस्त्रिकं क्षीर घृताश्यासदिकम्।
(सुश्रुत चिकित्सा-२७/१-डल्हण)

३. पुनश्च द्विविधं संशोधन संशमन भेदेन।
(सुश्रुत चिकित्सा-२७/१-डल्हण)

४. चरक चिकित्सा-१/४/३०-३५.

(ii) *Adravya Bhūta Rasāyana* (Non-pharmacological *Rasāyana*)

6. According to *Pāda Bheda*[1]

(i) *Abhyāmalkī Rasāyana Pāda*—6

(ii) *Prāṅakāmīya Rasāyana Pāda*—36

(iii) *Kara Pracitīya Rasāyana Pāda*—16

(iv) *Āyurveda Saṁutthānīya Rasāyana Pāda* —4

Relevant details of these types of *Rasāyana* are described below. As per the need, indications or contra indications these different types of *Rasāyana* may be used judiciously. If the *Rasāyana* Therapy is administered as per the norms laid down for it, extremely good response of the therapy is obtained.

1. According to Mode of Administration of *Rasāyana*

As already stated in *Caraka Samhitā* there are three methods described for administration of *Rasāyana* therapy, these are—

(i) *Kuti Prāveśika*

(ii) *Vātātapika*

(iii) *Droṅi Prāveśika*

(i) ***Kuti Prāveśika Rasāyana***[2] (Indoor Regimen)

It can be discussed under these steps—

(a) *Pūrva Karma*

(b) *Pradhāna Karma*

(c) *Pascāta Karma.*

---

१. चरक चिकित्सा-१/पाद-१-४.

२. चरक चिकित्सा-१/१/१७-२२.

(a) *Pūrva Karma*

Followings steps should be taken by a physician before the administration of *Rasāyana*. These include—

1. *Kuti Nirmāṅa*[1]

The *Kuti Prāveśika* procedure is a specialised indoor regimen of *Rasāyana* Therapy. The patient is to be placed in specially built "*Trigarbhā Kuti*" (Cottage), which should be constructed in a good site inhabited by the king, Physician, *Brāhmaṅas*, Saints and those who perform virtuous acts, a place which is free from alarm, which is worthy and where the required appliances can easily be procured.

This cottage should face towards the east or the north. It should be spacious in the plinth area and should have a high roof. It should have three concentric *Kutis (Trigarbhā Kuti)* and should be furnished with narrow ventilators. It's walls should be thick and it should be pleasant to reside in all seasons. It should be well lightened and pleasant to the mind and be free from undesirable noise etc. It should not be accessible to women. It should be equipped with all the required appliances. Physicians, Medicines and *Brahmins* should be readily available there.

2. Collection of Useful Material

Materials like Bed, *Āsana, Samśodhana Dravya, Rasāyana* drug, emergency drugs and medicines to treat complications, if any, should be collected in the cottage.

---

१. पुरे प्राप्योपकरणे हम्र्यनिर्वातनिर्भये।
दिश्युदीच्यां शुभे देशे त्रिगर्भा सूक्ष्मलोचनाम्।।
धूमातपरजोव्यालस्त्रीमूर्खाद्यविलङ्घिताम्।
सज्जवैद्योपकरणां सुमृष्टां कायरेत् कुटीम्।।
(अष्टांग हृदय उत्तर तन्त्र-३९/६-७)

3. Selection of *Rasāyana* Drugs

According to principles of *Āyurveda*, the *Rasāyana* drugs to be used in subjects should be selected in consideration of Age, individual constitution, adaptability, digestive capacity, the metabolic status and the state of body tissues. *Āyurveda* advocates the use of different *Rasāyana* drugs for the persons of different age group & different constitution etc.

The following tables illustrate the usefulness of various *Rasāyana* drugs in different age groups and for different indications.

(i) According to Age[1]

SN.	Age Group in Years	Desired Effect	*Rasāyana* Drugs
1.	1-10	*Bālya*	*Vacā, Kāsmari, Suvarṅa*
2.	11-20	*Vriddhī*	*Kāsmari, Aświagandhā, Balā*
3.	21-30	*Chavi*	*Lauha, Āmalakī*
4.	31-40	*Medhā*	*Śankhapuṣpī, Brāhmī, Jyotiṣmatī.*
5.	41-50	*Twaka*	*Jyotiṣmatī, Priyāla, Somarājī, Bhṛngarāja*
6.	51-60	*Dṛṣṭi*	*Jyotiṣmatī, Triphalā, Lauha, Śatāwari, Āmalakī*
7.	61-70	*Śukra*	*Ātmagupta, Vājikaraṅa* drugs
8.	71-80	*Vikrama*	Drugs may not be effective
9.	81-90	*Buddhi*	
10.	91-100	*Karmendriya*	

१. बाल्यं वृद्धिश्छविर्मेधात्वग्दृष्टि: शुक्र विक्रमौ।
बुद्धि कर्मेन्द्रियं चेतो जीवितं दशतो ह्रसेत।।
(शारंगधर संहिता पूर्वखण्ड ६/२०)

(ii) According to *Deha Prakṛti* (Constitution)—

Different types of *Rasāyana* drugs are needed by the persons of different types of *Prakṛti* or constitution as shown in table[1]

SN.	*Prakṛti*	***Rasāyana*** **Drugs**
1.	*Vāta*	*Balā, Nāgabala* with *Ghṛta*
2.	*Pitta*	*Āmalakī, Śatawarī*
3.	*Kapha*	*Bhallātaka, Rāsnā, Guggulu, Pippali*

(iii) According to *Sātmya*[2] (*Ṛtu Sātmya*-Seasonal Adaptability)

SN.	***Ṛtu/Kāla***	***Rasāyana*** **Drugs**
1.	*Ādāna Kāla* (February-July)	*Śita Vīrya and Laghu guṅa Dravya e.g. Āmalaki*
2.	*Visarga Kāla* (August-January)	*Uṣṅa Vīrya and Guru Guṅa Dravya e.g. Bhallātaka*

---

१. एते दशविधास्त्वेषां प्रयोगा: परिकीर्तिता:।
रोगप्रकृतिसात्म्यज्ञस्तान् प्रयोगान् प्रकल्पयेत्।।

(चरक चिकित्सा-१/२/१८)

२. तस्यां रसायनार्थी शरद वसन्ते वा शुक्लपक्षे प्रशस्तेऽहनि।

(अष्टाङ्ग संग्रह उत्तर तन्त्र-४९/१२)

Various *Rasāyana* Drugs Used in different *Ṛtus* (Seasons)

SN.	***Ṛtu* (Season)**	**Months**	**Condition of *Doṣās***	**Recommended *Rasāyana***
1.	*Hemanta*	December-January (*Śīrṣa-Poṣa*)	*Kapha Sancaya Pitta Śamana Vāta Prakopa*	*Dugdha, Ghṛta, Agru Lepa, Madhu, Yaṣṭi madhu, Bhallātaka, Balā, Atibalā, Pārada, Aśwagandhā etc.*
2.	*Śiśira*	February-March (*Māgha-Phālguna*)	*Kapha Sancaya Vāta Prakopa*	*Dugdha, Ghṛta, Madhu yaṣṭi, Balā, Bhallātaka, Atibalā, Nāgȧbalā, Pārada, Gambhārī etc.*
3.	*Vasanta*	April-May (*Caitra-Vaiśākha*)	*Kapha Prakopa*	*Brahatī, Pāthā, Bhringarāja, Tulasī, Candana, Harītakī, Śankha-puṣpi, Pippalī, Śilājatu, Kākamacī etc.*
4.	*Grṣama*	June-July (*Jayeṣṭha-Āṣāṛa*)	*Kapha Prakopa*	*Vidāri Kanda, Suvarṇa, Gokhṛu, Madhuyaṣṭi, Balā, Atibalā, Dugdha, Ghṛta etc.*
5.	*Varṣā*	August-September (*Śrāvana-Bhādrapada*)	*Pitta-Sancaya*	*Bhallātaka, Madhu, Pipallī, Citraka, Cavya, Harītakī, Pārada etc.*
6.	*Śarada*	October-November (*Āśvina-Kārtika*)	*Pitta Prakopa Vāta Śamana*	*Mandūkaparṇī, Vidāri Kanda, Āmalakī, Uśīra, Nāgabalā, Ghṛta, Suvarṇa etc.*

(iv) According to *Deśa Sātmya*

SN.	*Deśa*	*Rasāyana* Drugs
1.	*Sādhāraṅa*	*Sādhāraṅa* Drugs
2.	*Jāngala*	*Snigdha Uṣṅa* Drugs
3.	*Ānūpa*	*Rukṣa* Drugs.

(v) According to *Dhātu*

SN.	*Dhātu*	*Rasāyana Dravya*
1.	*Rasa*	*Khajūra, Drākṣā, Kāsmarī*
2.	*Rakta*	*Lauha, Āmalakī, Plāndu, Bhringarāja*
3.	*Māmsa*	*Balā, Nāgbalā, Rudantī, Aśwagandhā, Śālparṇī.*
4.	*Meda*	*Guggulu, Śīlājīta, Amṛtā, Haritakī*
5.	*Asthi*	*Lakṣā, Vanśalocana*
6.	*Majjā*	*Lauha, Vasā, Majjā*
7.	*Śukra*	*Ātmaguptā, Vājikaraṅa* drugs

(vi) According to *Srotasa*

1. *Rasāyana* Drugs beneficial for *Srotasa*

(i) *Pippalī*

(ii) *Bhallātaka*

(iii) *Guggulu*

(iv) *Rasona*

(v) *Kastūrī*

(vi) *Rudantī*.

(vii) According to *Ojas*

Pippali, Jīvanīya group of drugs.

(viii) According to *Agni*

S.N.	*Agni*	*Rasāyana* Drugs
1.	*Jāṭharāgni*	*Vidanga, Citraka, Pippalī, Haritakī*
2.	*Dhātwāgni*	*Āmalakī, Amritā, Kumarī, Pippalī*

2. *Rasāyana* Drugs Beneficial for *Agni*

(a) *Beneficial* for *Jaṭharāgni*

(i) *Vidanga*

(ii) *Haritakī*

(iii) *Pippalī*

(iv) *Citraka*

(b) Beneficial for *Dhātwāgni*

(i) *Āmalakī*

(ii) *Amṛtā*

(iii) *Kumārī*

(iv) *Pippali*

(c) *Agnivardhaka Rasāynopaga* Drugs

(i) *Suvarṅa*

(ii) *Kastūrī*

(iii) *Makaradhwaja*

(iv) *Kupilu*

(v) *Abhraka*

4. Preparation of the Patient

The following rules should be followed by a physician to prepare a person who has to undergo *Rasāyana* Therapy—

(i) *Yogya-Ayogya Vicāra*

(a). ***Vaya***—*Rasāyana* Therapy should be administered to a person in their early or middle age.[1]

(b) *Rasāyana* Therapy should be administered to those who have undergone oleation, blood letting and purification therapies.

(c) *Rasāyana* Therapy should be administered to those who are free of all encumberances and who can afford all the paraphernalia required.

(ii) *Rasāyana Sevana Yogya Kāla*[2]

Suitable *Kāla* (time) for *Rasāyana sevana* is also described by *Ācāryās* i.e. *Śarada, Basanta, Prāvṛta Ṛtu* are supposed to be the best period for administration of *Rasāyana* therapy because these *Ṛtus* provide *Śamaśitoṣṇa Kāla* i.e. which is neither too cold nor too hot, but is comfortable period for the patients.

---

१. पूर्वेवयसि मध्ये वा मनुष्यस्य रसायनम्।

(सुश्रुत चिकित्सा-२७/१)

२. अथोदगयने शुक्ले तिथिनक्षत्रपूजिते।

(चरक चिकित्सा-१/१/२१)

(iii) *Mātrā Nirdhāraṅa* (Dose Assessment)

Ācārya Caraka has emphasized that the dose of *Rasāyana* drug should be decided according to the "*Agnibala*" of the subject. It is further clarified by him that dose is ideal for the subject which does not interfere in his routine diet. *Aruṅadatta* has emphasized that nocturnal diet (Dinner) should not be disturbed due to the dose of *Rasāyana* Drugs.

Other scholars are of the opinion that the *Rasāyana* Drug should be administered in the morning in that much amount which should be digested by lunch time.

But in case of '*Vardhamāna-Rasāyana*', similar dose of *Rasāyana* drugs is to be administered in different persons e.g. *Pīpallī Vardhamāna Rasāyana*.

5. Rules for *Kuti Praveśa*

(i) A person desirous of undergoing Rejuvenation therapy should enter the *kuti* (cottage) on an auspicious day with an auspicious *Nakṣatra* and favourite *Muhurata* during the sun's northern course in the lighted half of the month (*Śukla Pakṣa*)[1]

(ii) A person should enter the cottage after shaving, endowed with the perserverance and memory, full of faith, single minded, having removed all afflictions, cherishing good will for all living beings, having worshiped the Gods and *Brāhamans* and having performed the *Pradakṣiṅā* of the Gods, Cow and *Brāhmans*.

---

१. अथोदगयने शुक्ले तिथिनक्षत्रपूजिते ....।
...... देवगोब्राह्मणान् कृत्वां ततस्तां प्रविशेत कुटीम्।।
(चरक चिकित्सा-१/१/२१-२३)

6. Necessity of *Samśodhana*

Before administration of *Rasāyana* Therapy to an individual, he has to undergo an appropriate *Samśodhana Karma* (Purificatory *Therapy*)[1] for perfect and adequate *Rasāyana* effects.

Samśodhana Yoga

The person who has undergone *Snehana* (oleation Therapy) and *Swedana* (fomentation) therapies earlier, should drink hot water added with the paste of *Haritakī*, *Āmalakī*, *Saindhava*, *Śunthī* (*Nāgar*), *Vacā*, *Haridrā*, *Pippalī* and *Guḍha* (Jaggery). By administering this preparation, he purges without any difficulty.[2]

7. *Samsarjana Karma*

The person who has thus been purified and who has followed the *Samsarjana karma* (Regimen of liquid diet after purification) should be given food prepared from *yava* only added with *ghee* for three (*Avara Śuddhi*), five (*Madhyama Śuddhi*) and seven days (*Uttama Śuddhi*) till the old faeces gets purified.[3]

---

१. तस्यां संशोधनैः शुद्धः सुखी जातबलः पुनः।
रसायनं प्रयुञ्जीत तत्प्रवक्ष्यामि शोधनम्।।
(चरक चिकित्सा-१/१/२४)

२. हरीतकीनां चूर्णानि सैन्धवामलके गुड़म्।
वचां विडंग रजनीं पिप्पलीं विश्वभेषजम्।
पिबेदुष्णाम्बुना जन्तुः स्नेह स्वेदोपपादितः।
तेन शुद्धशरीराय कृतसंसर्जनाय च।।
(चरक चिकित्सा-१/१/२५-२६)

३. त्रिरात्रं यावकं दद्यात् पञ्चाहं वाऽपि सर्पिषा।
सप्ताहं वा पुराणस्य यावच्छुद्धेस्तु वर्चसः।।
शुद्ध कोष्ठं तु तं ज्ञात्वा रसायनमुपाचरेत्।
वयःप्रकृतिसात्म्यज्ञो यौगिकं यस्य यद्भवेत्।।
(चरक चिकित्सा-१/१/२७-२८)

Having conditioned the alimentary tract in this manner the person should begin to consume that *Rasāyana* preparation which ever formula is found suitable after considering his habits.

(b) *Pradhāna Karma*

After proper purification,when patient is happy and has regained his strength, the *Rasāyana* drug should be administered. It is stated that *Kutiprāveśika* regimen is far too difficult to accomplish, but it is more useful than the other method.[1] So special eligibility qualities of persons are also spelt out for this method of *Rasāyana* Therapy. It appears that this method is really meant for positive health medicine. *Ācārya Caraka* and *Vāgabhatta* have given specific list of *Rasāyana* preparations which are to be administered by *kutiprāveśika* method for getting best results. These include—

(i) *Brahma Rasāyana*[2]

(ii) *Haritkyādi Rasāyana*[3]

(iii) *Āmalki Rasāyana*[4]

(iv) *Cayavanaprāśa Rasāyana*[5]

Management of Complications

Kutiprāveśika method is no doubt better, but is very difficult. If during the therapy, some complications arise

---

१. तयो: श्रेष्ठतर: पूर्वो विधि: स तु सुदुष्कर:।
(चरक चिकित्सा-१/४/२८)

२. चरक चिकित्सा-१/१/४१-५७, अष्टाङ्ग हृदय उत्तर तन्त्र-३९/१५-२३.

३. चरक चिकित्सा-१/१/७६, अष्टाङ्ग हृदय उत्तर तन्त्र ३९/२४-२७.

४. चरक चिकित्सा-१/१/७५, अष्टाङ्ग हृदय उनर तन्त्र ३९/२८-३२.

५. चरक चिकित्सा-१/१/५९-६९, अष्टाङ्ग हृदय उत्तर तन्त्र ३९/३३-४१.

due to faulty methods, proper respective treatment is to be provided to the subject, stopping the *Rasāyana* course.[1]

(c) *Pascāta Karma*

1. A Person should follow the instructions of the treating physician after the completion of *Rasāyana* Therapy in reference to *Āhāra, Vihāra* and *Ācāra* as discussed below–

(i) *Āhāra* (Dietary Restrictions)

Ācārya Caraka has advised to take specific *Pathya* after administration of *Rasāyana* therapy i.e. *Śāliṣaṣṭika Anna*,[2] with *ghee* and milk and *Ajā dugdha* (Goat's milk)[3] and *Sātmya Āhāra*.[4] Patient should be allowed to return to normal diet after double the time of *Rasāyana Sevana Kāla (Parihāra Kāla)*.[5] During this period the patient should remain on *laghu āhāra*, milk or other *Pathya dravyās*, otherwise *Mandāgni* may be produced.

(ii) *Vihāra*[6] (Life Style)

(a) Patient should avoid exertion.

---

१. रसायन विधि भ्रंशाज्जायेरन् व्याधयो यदि।
यथास्वमौषधं तेषां कार्य मुकत्वा रसायनम्।।
(चरक चिकित्सा-१/४/२९)

२. जीर्णे च षष्टिकं पयसा ससर्पिष्कमुपसेवमानो यथोक्तान गुणान् समश्नुत इति। (चरक चिकित्सा-१/१/५८)
जीर्णे च क्षीरसर्पिभ्यां शालिषष्टिकमश्नीयात्। (चरक चिकित्सा-१/२/११)

३. तस्याजं पयः प्रत्यवस्थापनम्। (चरक चिकित्सा १/४/७)

४. सात्म्यापेक्षरचाहार विधि।

५. द्विस्तावदग्निबलमभिसमीक्ष्य, प्रतिभोजनं यूषेण पयसा वा षष्टिकः ससर्पिप्कः।
(चरक चिकित्सा-१/१/७५)

६. रसायनं पीतवांस्तु निवाते तन्मनाः शुचिः।
आसीत् तिष्ठेच्च क्रामेच्च न कथञ्चन सविशेत्।।
(सुश्रुत चिकित्सा २९/११)

(b) He should avoid exposure to direct air, sunlight and cold air immediately after the *Rasāyana* Therapy.

(c) Mental stress should be avoided.

(iii) *Ācāra* (Psycho Social Codes & Conducts of Life)

Following three things are included in *Ācāra Vayavasthā* after administration of *Rasāyana* Therapy for obtaining better results of the therapy—

(a) Personal behaviour

(b) Social behaviour

(c) *Sātvika* behaviour

These aspects will be discussed is details under *Ācāra Rasāyana*.

2. *Niṣkramaṅa Vidhi* (To Come out of *Kuṭi*) No specific description is available in *Caraka* about *Niṣkramaṅa vidhi*, but *Ācārya Suśruta* has described it which is as follows—

(i) Following the same principles as followed during the time of entering the cottage, as auspicious day, favourite *Muhurata* especiality in *Purṅīmā*, the patient is instructed to come out of the "*Trigarbhā Kuti.*"[1]

(ii) *Suśruta* has indicated that it takes one month for the subject to remain in the cottage, i.e. ten days in one

---

१. ततश्चतुर्थेमासे पौर्णमास्यां शुचौ देशे ब्राह्मणानर्चयित्वा कृत मंगलो निष्क्रम्य यथोक्तं व्रजेदिति।

(सुश्रुत चिकित्सा-२९/१३)

यथा सुखविहारः काम भक्ष्यः स्यात्।

(चरक चिकित्सा-१/१/७५)

kuti. During this period the patient has to perform all his activities inside the *Kuti* until the outside environment becomes favourable. It is very important to maintain the internal environment of the body while the patient leaves the *Kuti*.

(ii) *Vātātapika Rasāyana* (Out Door Regimen)

Those individuals who cannot afford the time or other paraphernalia should be recommended *Vātātapika Rasāyana* or *Saurya Mārutika Rasāyana*.[1]

In *Vātātapika* procedure the person remains in his natural surroundings, freely moves in normal air and sun and continues to perform his daily normal schedule while under the therapy. It is convenient and cheap therapy but is less effective so far its *Rasāyana* effects are concerned.

Various *Rasāyana* formulations can be consumed by people under this therapy, which do not harm the body even if one walks in sun or air.

Vātātapika Sevana Yogya

This therapy is recommended to those people who cannot afford this much of time, having physical and mental stress and poor persons who do not have the resources essential for *Rasāyana* Therapy.

Ācārya Vāgabhatta has recommended the list of *Vātātapika Rasāyana Yogās*[2] which include *Śitodaka* (Cold

---

१. समर्थानामरोगाणां धीमतां नियतात्मनाम्।
कुटीप्रवेशः क्षणिनां परिच्छदवतां हितः।।
अतोऽन्यथा तु ये तेषां सौर्यमारुतिको विधिः।
(चरक चिकित्सा-१/४/२७, २८)

२. शीतोदकं पयः क्षौद्रं घृतमेकैकशो द्विशः।
त्रिशः समस्तमथवा प्राक पीतं स्थापयेद्वयः।।
(अष्टाङ्ग हृदय उत्तर तंत्र-३९/१४५)

water), milk, honey and *Ghee*. Thus following preperations can be used as *Vātātapika Rasāyana* preparations—

(i) *Śitodaka Rasāyana* (Cold Water)

(ii) Milk

(iii) Honey + *Ghee* in uneven ratio, separately or together.

(iv) *Harītakī Yoga*—Consuming two *Harītakī* daily with either Jaggery, Honey, *Śunthi* or *Lavaṅa*. The subject lives for hundred years.[1]

(v) *Āmalakī swarasa*[2]

(vi) *Āmalakī Cūrṅa*[3]

(vii) *Triphalā Rasāyana*[4]

(iii) *Droṅī Prāveśika Rasāyana* (Special Regimen)

This is a specialized procedure of *Rasāyana* Therapy used for recipe of "*Divya Rasāyana*" (Celestial Drugs). These drugs are used for rejuvenation and have wonderful impact over the body. Some of these drugs are *Brahma*, *Suvarcala, Ādityaparnī, Nāri, Soma, Padma, Aja* etc.[5]

In this procedure the person undergoing *Rasāyana* Therapy should be given *Śwarasa* (Juice) of all or anyone of the above mentioned drugs to the full of his stomach.

---

१. अष्टाङ्ग हृदय उत्तर तन्त्र-३९/१४६

२. अष्टाङ्ग हृदय उत्तर तन्त्र-३९/१४८

३. अष्टाङ्ग हृदय उत्तर तन्त्र-३९/१४९

४. चरक चिकित्सा-१/३/४१-४७.

५. ब्रह्मसुर्वचला नामौषधिर्यां.............।
........दशवर्षसहस्राण्यायुरनुपद्रवं चेति।।
(चरक चिकित्सा-१/४/७)

A *Droṅī* prepared from the green wood of "*Palāśa*" should be smeared with *Sneha* (*Ghee* or Oil). The person should be asked to remove all his clothes and sleep in this *Droṅī*.

He should then be covered with lid. After sometime person becomes unconscious. He regains consciousness after six months. After the person regains the consciousness he should be fed with goat's milk. It is described that within that six months he gets youthfulness, complexion, melodious voice, good shape, strength and lusture like God's. He develops mastery over his speech i.e. what he says comes true. He is endowed with the divine vision and hearing. He can walk for one thousand *Yojana* (Very long distance). He lives for Ten thousand years free from all obstacles.

But it is mentioned that only the sages can withstand the specific action of the *Divya auṣhadhis* not others who are devoid of self control. But persons in '*Vānaprastha āśrama*' and '*Grahastāśrama*' can also use these drugs provided they are sincere and have self control.[1]

According to Purpose of Administration of *Rasāyana*

Following types of *Rasāyana* can be grouped under this heading—

---

१. दिव्यानामोषधीनां यः प्रभावः स भवद्विधैः।
शक्यः सोढुमक्यस्तु स्यात् सोढुयकृतात्मभिः।।
औषधीनां प्रभावेण तिष्ठतां स्वे च कर्मणि।
भवतां निखिलंश्रेयः सर्वमेवोपपस्यिते।।
वानप्रस्थैर्गृहस्थैश्च प्रयतैर्नियतात्मभिः।
शक्या औषधयो ह्येताः सेवितुं विषयाभिजाः।।
(चरक चिकित्सा-१/४/८-१०)

(a) ***Kāmya Rasāyana*** (Promoter of normal health)

(i) *Prāṅa Kāmya* (Promoter of life-vitality and longevity)

(ii) *Medhā Kāmya* (Promoter of intellect)

(iii) *Sri Kāmya* (Promoter of Complexion and lusture)

(b) ***Naimittika Rasāyana*** (Promotion of specific vitality in specific diseases)

(c) ***Ājasrika Rasāyana*** (Dietary *Rasāyana*)

A. *Kāmya Rasāyana*[1]

The *Rasāyana* used in healthy persons for maintainance and promotion of positive health are known as *Kāmya Rasāyana*. *Kāmya Rasāyana* is indicated in health to promote vigour & vitality. It is categorized in following three types.[2]

(i) *Prāṅa Kāmya* (Promoter of life vitality and longevity) e.g. *Triphalā Rasāyana*, *Harītakī Rasāyana*.

(ii) *Medhā Kāmya* (Promoter of intellect and Mental Functions) e.g. *Brāhmī, Śankhpuṣpī*.

(iii) *Srikāmya* (Promoter of strength, vigour, complexion and lusture etc.) e.g. Āmalkī *Rasāyana*, *Loha Rasāyana*.

---

१. प्राण क्रोधाकाय: श्रीकाम इत्यादिकं काम्यं।

(सुश्रुत चिकित्सा २७/१-डल्हण)

२. भैषजाश्रितानां रसवीर्य विपाक प्रभावाणामायुर्बलवीर्य दोढ़र्याणां वय: स्थैर्यकराणामयनं लाभोपाये रसायनम्।।

(सुश्रुत चिकित्सा-२७/१-डल्हण)

(iv) There are some other classification of *Rasāyana* which are described by *Ācārya Suśruta*, which can also be grouped under *Kāmya Rasāyana*. These include—

(a) *Sarvopaghāta Śamnīya Rasāyana*

(b) *Medhāyuṣkāmīya Rasāyana*

(c) *Swabhāva Vyādhi Pratiṣedhanīya Rasāyana*

(d) *Nivṛtta Santāpīya Rasāyana*

(e) *Kṣhiṅa Balīya Rasāyana*

(f) *Vṛṣya Rasāyana*

(g) *Vājikaraṅa Rasāyana*.

(a) *Sarvopaghāta Śamnīya Rasāyana*

These are the recipes and modes of using elixers and rejuvenators of human organism which will make it invulnerable to the in roads of any disease or of decay e.g. *Cayavanaprāśa*.[1]

(b) *Medhāyuṣkamīya Rasāyana*[2]

Principaly all *Rasāyana* agents are supposed to promote both the body and the mind and as such promotion of *Medhā* i.e. intellect is an important attribute of *Rasāyana*. However the *Āyurvedic* texts describe certain *Rasāyana* drugs which specially influence the *Medhā* and promote mental competence. Such *Rasāyanās* are called *Medhya Rasāyana* which promote *Prajñā* (*Dhi, Dhṛti, Smṛti* i.e. intelligence and memory). Moreover *Suśruta* has described certain '*Divya-Rasāyanās* (Divine Remedies)

१. सुश्रुत चिकित्सा-२७.

२. सुश्रुत चिकित्सा-२८.

which has been claimed to afford total mental transformation and to impart divinity and super normal powers to man including the *Siddhis* and *Aiśvaryās* achievable by higher *Yogic* practices. However, in present times such *Divya Rasāyanās* are practically lost but the *Medhya Rasāyanās* are available.

Caraka has described four types of *Medhya Rasāyana*[1] namely,

1. *Swarasa* of *Mandūkaparnī*
2. Powder of *Yaṣṭimadhu* with milk
3. *Guduci Swarasa*
4. *Kalka* (paste) of *Śankhapuṣpī*

A number of other drugs have also been attributed with *medhya* effect. Many such drugs have been scientifically studied in recent years and they have been reported to possess varying degree of anxiolytic activity besides restoration of intelligence, memory and other nootropic effects.

Literally '*Medhya*' means anything which is beneficial for '*Medha*', which consists of—

(i) *Dhī* (Intelligence)

(ii) *Dhritī* (Power of Retention)

(iii) *Smṛti* (Memory)

These *Medhya Rasāyanās* have beneficial effects more prominently over mind. It improves the mental functions and intellect.

---

१. मण्डूकपर्ण्याः स्वरसः प्रयोज्यः क्षीरेण यष्टीमधुकस्य चूर्णम्।
रसो गुडुच्यास्तु समूल पुष्प्याः कल्कः प्रयोज्यः खलु शंखपुष्प्याः।।
(चरक चिकित्सा-१/३/३०-३१)

It is postulated that *Medhya Rasāyanās* and *Medhya* drugs described in *Āyurveda* may possess brain tonic effect, and promote natural tranquility of mind and mental competence. Studies on popular *medhya* drugs like *Śankhapuṣpī*, *Brāhmī, Madūkaparṇī* and *Aśwagandhā* have shown that these drugs act like mild to moderate anxiolytic agents and adaptogens. These drugs also produce a variety of psycho biological changes in the body which may be responsible for the *Medhya* effect of these drugs. Studies have shown that *Medhya Rasāyana* drugs of *Āyurveda* produce a variety of Psycho biological changes and beneficial effects, helping an individual to sustain and adopt in stress and senesence.

Pharmacodynamics of *Medhya* Drugs

To assess the pharmacodynamics of *Medhya* Drugs, a systematic literary survey was launched on *Medhya* Drugs by Certain *Āyurvedic* scholars. It was found that *Medhya* Drugs appear to be predominantly *Śīta Vīrya*, *Tikta* and *Madhura Rasa* dominant. Incidence of *katu*, *Amla*, *Lavaṅa Rasa* is least in *Medhya* Drugs. *Snigdha* and *Laghu Guṅās* are in highest incidence in these drugs.

Medhya drugs are used for the treatment of psychological and psychosomatic diseases, where the object of therapy is to achieve a tranquility of mind. Modern researches carried out on seveal *Medhya* drugs like *Śankhapuṣpī, Brāhmī, Mandukaparṅī, Yaṣṭīmadhu, Jatāmānsī, Sarpagandhā, Vacā* and *Aśwagandhā* indicate that these drugs have varying degree of psychotropic actions.

Pharmacological Properties of Some *Medhya Rasāyana*

SN.	Drugs	*Rasa*	*Guṅa*	*Vīrya*	*Vipāka*	Prabhāva
1.	*Śankhapuṣpī*	*Katu, Tikta, Kaṣāya*	*Sara, Guru Snigdha, Picchila*	*Śīta*	*Madhura*	*Medhya*
2.	*Mandūkaparṅī*	*Tikta*	*Laghu, Sara*	*Śīta*	*Madhura*	*Medhya*
3.	*Madhuyaṣti*	*Madhura*	*Guru, Snigdha*	*Śīta*	*Madhura*	*Medhya*
4.	*Guduci*	*Tikta, Kaṣāya*	*Guru, Snigdha*	*Uṣṅa*	*Madhura*	*Medhya*
5.	*Vakucī*	*Katu, Tikta*	*Laghu, Rukṣa*	*Uṣṅa*	*Katu*	*Medhya*
6.	*Citraka*	*Katu*	*Laghu, Rukṣa Tikṣaṅa*	*Uṣṅa*	*Katu*	*Medhya*
7.	*Aśwagandhā*	*Madhura, Tikta, Kaṣāya*	*Laghu, Snigdha*	*Uṣṅa*	*Madhura*	*Medhya*
8.	*Vacā*	*Tikta, Katu*	*Laghu, Sara, Tikṣṅa*	*Uṣṅa*	*Katu*	*Medhya*
9.	*Suvarṅa*	*Madhura, Kaṣāya*	*Laghu, Snigdha*	*Śīta*	*Madhura*	*Medhya*
10.	*Brāhmī*	*Tikta*	*Laghu, Snigdha*	*Uṣṅa*	*Katu*	*Medhya*
11.	*Jyotiṣmatī*	*Katu, Tikta*	*Tikṣaṅa, Sara, Snigdha*	*Uṣṅa*	*Katu*	*Medhya*
12.	*Nīlotpala*	*Madhura Kaṣāya, Tikta*	*Laghu, Snigdha*	*Śīta*	*Madhura*	*Medhya*

(c) *Swabhāva Vyādhi Pratiṣedhanīya Rasāyana*

These are the restorative and the constructive agents (*Rasāyana* measures) to arrest innate morbific tendencies and decay which are decreptitude, death, hunger, thirst and sleep etc. e.g. *Cayavanaprāśa, Brahma Rasāyana* etc.[1]

(d) *Nivṛtta Santāpiya Rasāyana*

These are the tonics and remedies which remove mental and physical distress e.g. *Indrokta Rasāyana.*[2]

Some Examples of *Kāmya Rasāyana*

* *Prāṅakāmiya*	-	*Triphalā Rasāyana*
* *Medhāyuṣkāmiya*	-	*Brāhmī, Yaṣṭimadhu, Śankhapuṣpī, Guducī etc.*
* *Sarvopaghāta Śamṇīya*	-	*Cayavanaprāśa, Brahma Rasāyana*
* *Svābhāvika Vyādhi Pratiṣedhaniya*	-	*Cayavanaprāśa, Brahma Rasāyana*
* *Nivṛtta Santāpiya*	-	*Indrokta Rasāyaṅa*
* *Kṣiṅa Baliya*	-	*Śatāvarī Ghṛta*
* *Vṛṣya*	-	*Vṛṣya Gutikā*
* *Vājikaraṅa*	-	*Vṛṣya Pūplicā.*

(B) *Naimittika Rasāyana*

Promoter of specific vitality in specific diseases, certain *Rasāyanās* may be used in patients suffering from diseases in order to promote the vitality in the particular disease. This is called *Naimittika Rasāyana.*[3] *Śilājatu* and

---

१. सुश्रुत चिकित्सा-२९.

२. सुश्रुत चिकित्सा-३०.

३. पुनश्च त्रिविधं काम्यं नैमित्तिकम् आजस्रिकं च।

(सुश्रुत चिकित्सा-२७/१-डल्हण)

नैमित्तिकं व्याधिनिमित्तं शिलाजतु भल्लातक तुवरकादयम्....।

(सुश्रुत चिकित्सा-२७/१-डल्हण)

Tuvaraka are the specific examples of *Naimittika Rasāyana* for *Prameha* and *Kuṣṭha*.

The concept of *Naimittika Rasāyana* appears to be subsequent development in *Rasāyana Tantra* where specific *Rasāyanās* were conceived for use in patients of specific disease. This concept emerges in *Suśruta Samhitā* and is more clearly stated by *Ḍalhaṅa*. Specific role of certain *Rasāyanās* in the care and management of specific diseases such as *Śilājatu* in *Prameha* and *Tuvaraka* in *Kuṣṭha* is an unique idea and adds newer dimensions of *Rasāyana Tantra*. *Naimittika Rasāyana* is used in a diseased person as an adjunct to the specific therapy. Thus, it must be clear that *Naimittika Rasāyana* is not the specific medical treatment for a particular disease but it should be used as an adjunct to the specifc therapy. However in the present day society in our country where the curative medicine has still the priority over the positive health programmes the *Naimittika Rasāyanās* are of greater value.

In *Suśruta Samhitā* it has been postulated that the *Naimittika Rasāyana* approach is quite effective in the management of *Prameha Roga* with *Śilājatu Rasāyana* and *Kuṣṭha Roga* with *Tuvaraka Rasāyana*. The concept of *Naimittika Rasāyana* Therapy should be developed further and the list of *Naimittika Rasāyana* remedies may be enlarged by sorting out all such drugs which possess *Rasāyana* effect and have also specific effect on one or the other disease. It has been reported that *Aśwagandhā* can be used as a specific *Naimittika Rasāyana* agent in cases of *Apasmāra* (Epilepsy). Similarly *Bhallātaka* can be used as a *Naimittika Rasāyana* in cases of *Āmavāta* (Rh. Arthritis) with definite benefits. The *Naimittika Rasāyana* remedies may also be used as adjunct therapy along with specific modern treatment of different diseases with added advantage.

It has been reported that in the management of Tuberculosis with modern Chemo Therapy along with *Āyurvedic Naimittika Rasāyana* yielded encouraging results. This approach is worth popularising among the modern medical practitioners too.

Following are the popularly used *Naimittika Rasāyana* in specific diseases according to *Bṛhatatrayī*—

(a) In *Caraka Samhitā*

	Conditions/Diseases		***Naimittika Rasāyana***
(i)	*Raktā pitta*	-	*Gambhārī Phala*
(ii)	*Śoṣa*	-	*Nāgabalā*
(iii)	*Kuṣṭha, Kandu, Udarda*	-	*Bākucī*
(iv)	*Kuṣtha*	-	*Khadira*
(v)	*Unmāda*	-	*Brāhmī*
(vi)	*Apasmāra*	-	*Brāhmī*

(b)* In *Suśruta Samhitā

(i)	*Gulma, Pāndu, Grahṅī, Arśa, Kṣaya, Granthi Roga*	-	*Harītakī*
(ii)	*Kāsa, Śwāsa, Kṣaya, Hṛdroga*	-	*Cayavanaprāśa*
(iii)	*Kaphaghna, Agnivardhaka*	-	*Bhallātaka*

(c)* In *Vāgabhatta-Aṣṭānga Hṛdya

(i)	*Tridoṣaghna*	-	*Śilājīta, Kalihāri*
(ii)	*Kāsa, Śwāsa, Hṛdroga*	-	*Cayavanaprāśa*
(iii)	*Kuṣṭha*	-	*Tuvaraka, Bākucī*
(iv)	*Kāsa, Śwāsa, Yakṣamā, Arśa, Grahaṅī.*	-	*Pippalī*

Following are the popularly used *Naimittika Rasāyana* in specific diseases

SN.	Disease/Conditions	Proposed *Naimittika Rasāyana*
1.	*Dṛṣṭi Māndya*	*Jyotiṣmatī, Trīphalā, Śatāvarī, Yaṣṭimadhu.*
2.	*Kuṣṭha* and Skin Disorders	*Tuvaraka, Bhallātaka, Vīdanga, Somarājī, Gandhaka.*
3.	*Rājayakṣmā*	*Pippalī, Rasona, Nāgabalā, Śilājatu, Cayavanaprāśa.*
4.	*Śwāsa*	*Agastya Rasāyana, Bhallātaka*
5.	*Prameha*	*Śilājatu, Harīdrā, Āmalakī*
6.	*Hṛdroga*	*Śālparṅī, Arjuna*
7.	*Grahaṅī and Gulma Roga*	*Pippalī, Bhallātaka*
8.	*Pāndu*	*Lauha, Āmalakī*
9.	*Vāta Vyādhi*	*Rasona, Guggulu, Balā, Nāgabalā*
10.	*Medo Roga*	*Guggulu, Haritakī*
11.	Hypertension	*Medhya* Drugs, *Rāsnā, Balā, Rasona*
12.	Allergic Disorders	*Haridrā*
13.	Hypotension	*Kasturī, Kupilū*
14.	*Āmavāta*	*Amṛta Bhallātaka*
15.	*Śīta Pitta*	*Haridrā*

(c) *Ājasrika Rasāyana* (Dietary *Rasāyana*)

Ājasrika Rasāyana is the nutrition which is taken regularly as food,[1] e.g. Daily use of milk, *ghee*, fruits, *Vegādhāraṅa*, *Ahimsā* and *Brahmacarya*.

Thus *Rasāyana Dravyās* used in regular practices as food are called as *Ājasrika Rasāyana*. These things are being used by human beings in their routine life and it maintains an equilibrium of *Dhātus* in the body and body remains in a healthy state as a result all mental and physical activities are done in their proper manner.

3. According to Mode of Actions

According to their modes of actions, *Rasāyana* drugs are divided into two groups[2] as described below—

(i) *Samśodhana Rasāyana*

(ii) *Samśamana Rasāyana*.

(i) *Samśodhana Rasāyana*

The drugs used for the purpose of purification of body by the processes of *Vamana*, *Virecana* etc. can be included in this type of *Rasāyana*. By the use of *Rasāyana Dravyās* vitiated *Doṣās* can be enrouted out of the body which ultimately results in rejuvenation of body e.g. *Soma Rasāyana*.

(ii) *Samśamana Rasāyana*

By the use of this type of *Rasāyanās*, vitiated *Doṣās* are not expelled out of body, but get pacified inside the body. It is a group of divine drugs.

---

१. आजस्रिक क्षीर घृताभ्यासदिकम्।

(सुश्रुत चिकित्सा-२७/१-डल्हण)

२. पुनश्च द्विविधं संशोधन संशमन भेदेन।

(सुश्रुत चिकित्सा-२७/१-डल्हण)

Samśamana group of *Rasāyanās* are used in larger extent in comparison to *Samśodhana Rasāyanās* e.g. *Nāgabalā, Cayavanaprāśa, Brahma Rasāyana, Āmalakī Rasāyana, Bhringarāj, Guduci, Brāhmī, Bhallātaka, Pippalī, Gambhārī, Silājatu, Śankhapuṣpi, Triphalā Rasāyana, Yaṣṭīmadhu* and *Punarnava* etc. This type of *Rasāyana* drugs promote longevity, intellect, strength and lusture of the body. These *Rasāyanās* are used in a routine fashion.

4. *Ācāra Rasāyana* (Conduct *Rasāyana*)

Āyurveda identifies at least three distinct modalities of *Rasāyana* to optimise the cellular nutrition and there by to attain rejuvenation. These include—

(i) *Āhāra Rasāyana* (Dietary Modalities)

(ii) *Ācāra Rasāyana* (Behavioural Modalities)

(iii) *Dravya Rasāyana* (Drug Based Measures)

(i) *Āhāra Rasāyana* (Dietary Modalities)

The quality of nutrition plays an important role in the process of ensuring optimum nutrition at cellular levels. If the diet is wholesome and compatible, the end products emanating from its digestion i.e. *Āhāra Rasa* (essence of food) shall be adequately dynamic to penetrate into the tissues. As already mentioned in *Caraka Samhitā* that the *Āhara Rasa* provides nutrition to *Rasa*, Plasma and such other fluid constituents of the body like *Rakta* (Erythrocyte), *Māmsa* (muscles), *Meda* (fat), *Asthi* (bone), *Majjā* (marrow), *Śukra* (semen), *Ojas*, the material constituents of the five sense organs which are the essence of the tissue elements, joints, ligaments and mucin etc. of the body. Therefore the selection of food is of paramount importance in the path of rejuvenation. In the state of equilibrium the wholesome and compatible diet which is responsible to produce pure *Āhāra Rasa* ultimately results in adequately dynamic tissue element.

In *Āyurvedic* text *Ācārya Dalhaṅa* in his commentary on *Suśruta Samhitā*, described this type of *Rasāyana* as *Ājasrika Rasāyana* where it is stated that in this type of *Rasāyana*, daily use of milk (*Dugdha*) and *Ghee* in diet enhances essence of tissue elements which ultimately rejuvenate the individuals.

(ii) ***Ācāra Rasāyana***[1] **(Behavioural Modalities)**

The quality of cellular nutrition is also greatly influenced by the behaviour of the individual and this behaviour embodies with somatic and psychic dimensions. For example, the significance of an exercise in *Rasāyana*. Well designed exercise programmes (*Yoga*) open up all the circulatory channels both at macro and micro levels. Thus the essence of food flows through the systems freely to

---

१. सत्यवादिनमक्रोधं निवृत्तं मद्यमैथुनात्।
अहिंसकमनायासं प्रशान्तं प्रियवादिनम्।।
जपशौचपरं धीरं दाननित्यं तपस्विनम्।
देवगोब्राह्मणाचार्य गुरुवृद्धार्चने रतम्।।
आनृशंस्यपरं नित्यं नित्यं करुणवेदिनम्।
समजागरणस्वप्नं नित्यं क्षीरघृताशिनम्।।
देशकालप्रमाणज्ञं युक्तिशमनहङ्कृतम्।
शस्ताचारमसंकीर्णमध्यात्मप्रवणेन्द्रियम्।।
उपासितारं वृद्धानामस्तिकानां जितात्मनाम्।
धर्मशास्त्रपरं विद्यान्नरं नित्यरसायनम्।।
गुणैरेतैः समुदितैः प्रयुङ्क्ते यो रसायनम्।
रसायनगुणान् सर्वान् यथोक्तान् स समश्नुते।।
(चरक चिकित्सा-१/४/३०-३५)

deliver the nutrients to all tissues. The psychic dimensions of these modalities emphasize on the positive mental attitudes. Traits like self-containment, love, compassion helping attitude etc. are considered in *Āyurveda* to work like *Rasāyana* and thereby down regulate aging process. Obviously, negative attitudes like anger, jealously, greed tend to cause a constriction of circulatory channels and thereby block the flow of nutrients. This can be well understood by the example of *Ajīrṅa* (indigestion) caused due to negative attitude. It is mentioned that if an individual is affected with grief, fear, anger, sorrow, excessive sleep and excessive vigil, wholesome food consumed in proper quantity may not be properly digested.

This emphasizes that positive attitude plays very important role in formation of essence of food. While describing *Ācāra Rasāyana Ācārya* mentions that the individual can attain all beneficial effects of *Rasāyana* only by following these behavioural modalities (good conducts). In *Caraka Samhitā* there is description of *Ācāra Rasāyana* in 4th *Pāda* (Part) of *Rasāyana* Chapter. *Ācārya Suśruta* has described it in different words. In the context of *Rasāyana* there are two types of psychosocial conducts, producing *Rasāyana Prabāva* in body, they are—

(i) *Buddhi-Medhā Vardhaka Gaṅa* (ii) *Āyuvardhaka Gaṅa*—which indicates, different types of psychosocial conducts may have (*Rasāyana*) beneficial effects on the mental faculties and longevity of the man.

In *Ācāra Rasāyana* broadly three things are included—

1. Personal behaviour
2. *Sātvika* behaviour
3. Social behaviour.

1. About *Personal behaviour, Ācārya Caraka* suggested that one should be devoid of alcohol and sex indulgence, one should not indulge in violence or over exhaustion, one should be peaceful and pleasing in his speech, one's awakening and sleeping time should be regular. One should take sufficient amount of *Dugdha* and *Ghṛta* habitually. One should be devoid of ego.

2. About *Sātvika behaviour Ācārya* have recommended that one should practice *Japa* (incantation) and cleanliness. One should become stable and steady (*Dhīra*). One should regularly practice charity and penance (*Tapa*). One should have love for spiritual knowledge. One should have reverence for seniors, *Āstikas* and persons having self control. One should regularly study scriptures i.e. should indulge in *Swādhāyaya*.

3. About *Social behaviour, Ācārya* have suggested that one should give donations and have sympathetic behaviour for others. One should regularly offer *seva* to Gods, Cows, *Brāhmṇās*, Teachers, Preceptors and old people. One should remain absolutely free from barbarious acts. One should be broad minded having knowledge of *Deśa, Kāla, Pramāṇa* and *Yukti* i.e. one should remain conscious about the change of body and environment.

Ācārya has suggested that if a person is having these qualities, he gets best result out of Rejuvenation Therapy and when practices Rejuvenation measures he attains all the Rejuvenation effects described in the text.

Thus it can be said that *Ācāra Rasāyana* is a preventive measure for physical and mental illness and to prevent premature aging. It can be kept in the category of *Daivavyapāsrayic Cikitsā* which is regularly practiceable regimen.

3. *Dravya Rasāyana* (Drug Based Measures)

Besides two personalised modalities, *Āyurveda* also finds a fairly good number of herbs as well as minerals which improve the quality of *Rasa* circulation in the body and these are grouped under *Rasāyana*. While considering the subject of Rejuvenation Therapies—these are unintentionally labelled as Rejuvenators.

These *Rasāyana* drugs may be used as a single or as compound drugs.

These single or compound *Rasāyana* drugs may be used by *Kutipraveśika* method or by *Vātātapika* Method.

And some of these drugs are meant for *Kāmya Rasāyana* while some other are meant for *Naimittika Rasāyana*.

Again some of these are meant for *Samśodhana Rasāyana* and some others are meant for *Samśamana Rasāyana*.

4. According to *Bheṣja Bheda*

(According to Drugs/Measures Used)

This is of two types—

(i) *Dravya Bhūta Rasāyana* (Drug *Rasāyana*)

(ii) *Adravya Bhūta Rasāyana* (Non-pharmacological *Rasāyana*)

(i) *Dravya Bhūta Rasāyana*

Single or compound drugs may be used as *Rasāyana* e.g. *Haritakī, Āmalakī, Pippalī, Nāgbalā, Rasonā, Bhallātaka* etc.

(ii) *Adravya Bhūta Rasāyana*

Some behaviour embodies which act as *Rasāyana*

e.g.—*Ācāra Rasāyana, Yama, Niyama, Prāṇāyāma, Tapa, Yoga, Santoṣa* etc.

In the Allopathic system of medicine Dr. Alexis Carra in his book entitled "Man the unknown (Chapter V)" has written about types of Rejuvenation as below—

1. In this type of rejuvenation, the person is changed incompletely and his mental stage is unaltered. His memory will be good, there will be changes in histological and humoral levels. Thus the experiences of the years can be utilized usefully.

2. The views of Steinach (1920) and Voronoff (1920) lead us to believe that the general state of the person will improve along with improvements in enthusiasm and virility.

Out of these views first is partly similiar to *Rasāyana*.

Method of Administration of *Rasāyana* Therapy

Before administration of *Rasāyana* Therapy to an individual he has to undergo an appropriate *Samśodhana Karma* (Purificatory therapy).[1]

In the text the term *Samśodhana* is used in plural. This implies that all the purificatory therapies *(Pancakarmās)* are to be administered to the individual. However only one type of elimination Therapy is described in some texts

---

१. तस्यां संशोधनैः शुद्धः सुखी जातबलः पुनः।
रसायनं प्रयुञ्जीत तत्प्रवक्ष्यामि शोधनम्।।
शुद्धकोष्ठं तु तं ज्ञात्वा रसायनमुपाचरेत्।
वयः प्रकृतिसात्म्यज्ञो यौगिकं यस्य यद्भवेत्।।
(चरक चिकित्सा-१/१/२४, २८)

because it is said to be specific for *Rasāyana* Therapy.[1] But in all other classical texts of *Āyurveda* proper cleansing of the individual is indicated with *Pancakarma* Therapy for perfect and adequate *Rasāyana* effects.

After the administration of the elimination Therapy, normally the patient becomes a little weak. Therefore proper diet (*Samsarjana Karma*) should be given to the patient. By this he will regain his strength. Similarly, the patient needs mental purification as well. Therefore, the patient should strictly follow a suitable code of psychosocial conduct as described under "*Ācāra Rasāyana.*" Such a procedure rejuvenates the individual.

About importance of these purificatory processes before administration of *Rasāyana* Therapy, *Acārya Suśruta* and *Vāgbhatta* have quoted one example that *Rasāyana* Therapy does not produce its desired effects in an unpurified body in the same way as a dirty cloth does not take up due brightness of colour on dyeing.[2]

---

१. हरीतकीनां चूर्णानि सैन्धवामलके गुडम्।
वचां विडङ्गं रजनीं पिप्पलीं विश्वभेषजम्।।
पिबेदुष्णाम्बुना जन्तुः स्नेहस्वेदोपपादितः।
तेन शुद्धशरीराय कृतसंसर्जाय च।।
त्रिरात्रं यावकं दद्यात् पञ्चाहं वाऽपि सर्पिषा।
सप्ताहं वा पुराणस्य यावच्छुद्धेस्तु वर्चसः।।
शुद्धकोष्ठं तु तं ज्ञात्वा रसायनमुपाचरेत्।
वयः प्रकृतिसात्म्यज्ञो यौगिकं यस्य यद्भवेत्।।
(चरक चिकित्सा-१/१/२५-२८)

२. नाविशुद्धशरीरस्य युक्ता रसायनो विधिः।
न भाति वाससि क्लिष्टे रङ्गयोग इवाहितः।।
(सुश्रुत चिकित्सा २७/४)

To gain complete effects of *Rasāyana* Therapy *Ācaryās* have described some *Pūrva Karma* before administration of *Rasāyana* Drug.

Nitya Rasāyana-Adravya Rasāyana—

The person who speaks the truth, who does not become angry, who engages his sense organs and mind in the pursuit of knowledge of soul etc. who is calm and who always indulges in good activities only should be considered as receiving *Nitya Rasāyana* (Daily Rejuvenatory Therapy).[1]

Benefits of *Rasāyana* Therapy—He who endowed with these qualities consumes the rejuvenatory recipes, becomes free from the bondage of birth & death, enjoys long life in this life & also in the next.[2]

Rasāyana Sevana Yogya* or *Ayogya

(Indication & Contraindication of *Rasāyana* Therapy)

It is mentioned in classics that *Rasāyana* therapy if administered improperly, it produces several hazardous effects.[3] So *Rasāyana* Therapy must be administered properly in proper persons.

---

१. सत्यवादिनमक्रोधमध्यात्मप्रवणेन्द्रियम्।
शान्तं सद्वृत्तनिरतं विद्यान्नित्यरसायनम्।।
(अष्टाङ्ग हृदय उत्तरतंत्र-३९/१७९)

२. गुणैरेभिः समुदितः सेवते यो रसायनम्
स निवृत्तात्मा दीर्घायुः परत्रेह च मोदते।।
(अष्टाङ्ग हृदय उत्तर तंत्र-३९/१८०)

३. समूल काषं तु कवन्ति देहं भ्रंशाद्विधेस्ते न विवर्जितानि।
(अष्टाङ्ग-संग्रह उत्तर तंत्र-४९/२५२)

1. Contraindications—*Ācārya Suśruta* has mentioned seven types of people in which *Rasāyana* Therapy should not be given.[1] They are the interpret, the lazy, the indigent, the careless, the immoral, the sinful and the trifler of medicine because of their respective ignorance, inactivity, poverty, vascillation, intemperance, impiety & inability to rescue the genuine medicine. Following persons should not be advised *Rasāyana* therapy—

1. ***Anātmavāna***—Those who do not have proper knowledge, idiot by nature should not be given this therapy.

2. ***Ālasi* (Lazy)**—This type of person avoids the *Rasāyana* Therapy and does not follow the rules strictly.

3. ***Daridra* (Poor)**—This type of person cannot afford the costly medicines, *Pathya* & the time for it.

4. ***Pramādi***—This type of persons are not steady minded & may not follow the rules & regulations strictly, which may lead to complications.

5. ***Vyasani***—Persons who are addicted to alcohol, gambling etc. can not be free for *Rasāyana*. He is said to be a servant of his addictions, thus is not able to undergo *Rasāyana* Therapy properly.

6. ***Pāpi***—The sinful persons do not follow the religion & their duties properly so they have been contra indicated for *Rasāyana*.

---

१. अथ खलु सप्त पुरुषाः रसायनं नोपयुञ्जीरन् तद्यथा-अनात्मवानलसो दरिद्रः प्रमादी व्यसनी पापकृद् भेषजापमानी चेति। सप्तभिरेव कारणैर्न सम्पद्यते, तद्यथा-अज्ञानादनारम्भादस्थिर चित्तत्वाद् दारिद्र्यादनायत्तत्वादधर्माद् औषधालाभाच्चेति।। (सुश्रुत चिकित्सा-३०/४)

7. ***Bhaiṣajāpamāni***—Those who don't have faith in medicine should not be given *Rasāyana* because the medicine may not produce proper effects in them. *Ācārya Caraka* supports this view by saying that persons who are with evil designs, who are not free from diseases, who are not *Dwijāti*. [*Brāhmaṇa, Kṣatṛya, Vaiṣya*], who have no faith in this therapy, should not be advised *Rasāyana* therapy.[1] *Ācārya Vāgbhatta* agrees with this view.

Indications :—In different contexts *Ācārya Caraka* has mentioned about certain persons to whom *Rasāyana* Therapy may be administered so as to obtain maximum effects of *Rasāyana*. These include—

1. The persons whose mind and body are clean and who are self controlled.[2]

2. The persons who are able bodied, whose bodies are free from diseases, who have intellect, who have sufficient time to spare & who have adequate wealth and faith in physician[3] & who have undergone purificatory therapies.

---

१. तदेतन्नं भवेद्वाच्यं सर्वमेव हतात्मसु।
अरूजेभ्योऽद्विजातिभ्य: शुश्रुषा येषु नास्ति च।।
(चरक चिकित्सा-१/४/३८)

२. योगा ह्यायु:प्रकर्षार्था जरारोग निवर्हणा:।
मन: शरीर शुद्धानां सिद्धयन्ति प्रयतात्मनाम्।।
(चरक चिकित्सा-१/४/३७)

३. समर्थानामरोगाणां धीमतां नियतात्मनाम्।
कुटीप्रवेश: क्षणिनां परिच्छदवतां हित:।।
(चरक चिकित्सा-१/४/२७)

3. According to *Ācārya Suśruta* & *Vāgbhatta* the maximum effects of the *Rasāyana* Therapy can be obtained only if it is used between 3rd & 5th decades of life.[1]

Pharmacodynamics of *Rasāyana* Drugs

A systematic study conducted by various scholars to work out the *Rasa*, *Guṅa*, *Vīrya*, *Vipāka* & *Prabhāva* of the known *Rasāyana* Drugs have revealed that most of the *Rasāyana* drugs are *Tikta* & *Madhura* in *Rasa*, some have *Katu* and *Kaṣāya Rasa*. Most of the *Rasāyana* drugs are *Laghu* in *Guṅa*, some are *Snigdha* & *Ruksha Guṅa* dominant. Similarly *Uṣṅa* & *Śīta Vīrya* drugs are equally common. *Rasāyana* drugs have *Madhura* & *Katu Vipāka* in equal preponderance.

Rasāyana drugs having *Madhura, Guru, Snighda* & *Śīta* properties act at the level of *Rasa* by improving the nutritional value of the *Poṣaka Rasa* which helps to obtain the best quality of *Dhātūs* viz. *Śatāvari, Balā, Yaṣṭimadhu, Āmalakī* etc. *Rasāyana* drugs with *Laghu-Guṇa, Uṣṇa Vīrya* & *Katu Rasa* may act at the level of *Agni* by improving metabolism, they improve the quality of *Dhātūs*. Similarly the drugs with *Katu, Tikta* & *Kaṣāya Rasa, Viśada, Rukṣa* & *Laghu guṇās, Uṣṅa Vīrya, Katu Vipāka* may cause *Srotośodhana* and thus inducing the *Rasāyana* effect. *Rasāyana* effect of a drug is governed by not only its *Guṇās*, but also by *Prabhāva* of these drugs.

---

१. पूर्वे वयसि मध्ये वा मनुष्यस्य रसायनम्।

(सुश्रुत चिकित्सा-२७/३)

Pharmacological Properties of Some *Rasāyana* Drugs

S.N.	Drug	*Rasa*	*Guṅa*	*Vīrya*	*Vipāka*
1.	*Haritakī*	*Madhura, Tikta, Kaṣāya, Katu, Amla*	*Rukṣa, Laghu*	*Uṣṅa*	*Madhura*
2.	*Āmalakī*	*Amla, Madhura, Kaṣāya*	*Laghu, Rukṣa, Sīta*	*Śita*	*Madhura*
3.	*Pippalī*	*Katu*	*Snighda, Laghu, Tikṣṇa*	*Anuṣṅa*	*Madhura*
4.	*Śilājatu*	*Katu, Tikta, Kaṣāya*	*Laghu, Rukṣa*	*Uṣṅa*	*Katu*
5.	*Kākamācī*	*Tikta*	*Laghu*	*Anuṣṅa-sīta*	*Katu*
6.	*Vidārikanda*	*Madhura*	*Snigdha*	*Śīta*	*Madhura*
7.	*Bhallātaka*	*Madhura, Kaṣāya*	*Laghu, Snigdha, Tikṣṇa*	*Uṣṅa*	*Madhura*
8.	*Lauha*	*Madhura, Tikta, Kaṣāya*	*Guru, Rukṣa*	*Śīta*	*Madhura*
9.	*Balā*	*Madhura*	*Snigdha*	*Śīta*	*Madhura*
10.	*Atibalā*	*Madhura*	*Snigdha*	*Śīta*	*Madhura*
11.	*Candana*	*Tikta, Madhrua*	*Rukṣa, Laghu*	*Śīta*	*Katu*
12.	*Agaru*	*Katu, Tikta,*	*Tikṣṇa, Laghu*	*Uṣṅa*	*Katu*
13.	*Dhava*	*Madhura, Kaṣāya*	*Rukṣa, Laghu*	*Śīta*	*Katu*
14.	*Tiniśa*	*Kaṣāya*	*Laghu, Rukṣa*	*Śīta*	*Katu*
15.	*Khadīra*	*Tikta, Kaṣāya*	*Laghu, Rukṣa*	*Śīta*	*Katu*
16.	*Śīśama*	*Katu, Tikta, Kaṣāya*	*Laghu, Rukṣa*	*Uṣṅa*	*Katu*
17.	*Asana (Vijayasāra)*	*Tikta, Kaṣāya*	*Laghu, Rukṣa*	*Uṣṅa*	*Katu*
18.	*Muktā (Rāsnā)*	*Tikta*	*Guru*	*Uṣṅa*	*Katu*

SN.	Drug	*Rasa*	*Guṅa*	*Vīrya*	*Vipāka*
19.	*Śveta (Aprājitā)*	*Katu, Tikta, Kaṣāya*		*Śīta*	*Katu*
20.	*Sthirā (Śalparṅī)*	*Tikta, Madhura*	*Guru, Snigdha*	*Uṣṅa*	*Madhura*
21.	*Punarnavā-Śveta*	*Madhura, Tikta*	*Laghu, Rukṣa*	*Uṣṅa*	*Madhura*
	Punarnavā-Rakta	*Kaṣāya, Tikta*	*Laghu, Rukṣa*	*Śīta*	*Katu*
22.	*Guggulu*	*Katu, Tikta, Kaṣāya*	*Viśada, Rukṣa, Laghu*	*Uṣṅa*	*Katu*
23.	*Atirasā (Śatāvarī)*	*Madhura, Tikta*	*Guru, Snigdha*	*Śīta*	*Madhura*
24.	*Nāgabalā*	*Madhura*	*Snigdha*	*Śīta*	*Madhura*
25.	*Dugdha*	*Madhura*	*Guru, Snigdha Mṛdu, Picchila*	*Śīta*	*Madhura*
26.	*Ghṛta*	*Madhura*	*Guru, Snigdha*	*Śīta*	*Madhura*
27.	*Kālamegha*	*Tikta*	*Laghu, Rukṣa Tikṣṇa*	*Uṣṅa*	*katu*
28.	*Gambhāri*	*Madhura, Tikta, Kaṣāya*	*Guru*	*Uṣṇa*	*Katu*
29.	*Vārāhi Kanda*	*Katu, Tikta. Madhura*	*Laghu, Snigdha*	*Uṣṇa*	*Katu*
30.	*24 Soma Rasāyana*	*Divya*			
31.	*18 Dravya Like Soma*	*Rasāyana*			
32.	*Tuvaraka*	*Tikta, Katu, Kaṣāya*	*Laghu, Snigdha, Tikṣṇa*	*Uṣṅa*	*Katu*
33.	*Jala*	*Avyakta*	*Laghu*	*Śīta*	

SN.	Drug	*Rasa*	*Guṅa*	*Vīrya*	*Vipāka*
34.	*Bṛahatī*	*Katu, Tikta*	*Laghu, Rukṣa, Tikṣna*	*Śīta*	*Katu*
35.	*Usīra*	*Tikta, Madhura*	*Rukṣa, Laghu*	*Śīta*	*katu*
36.	*Pāthā*	*Tikta*	*Laghu, Tikṣna*	*Uṣṅa*	*Katu*
37.	*Sārivā*	*Madhura, Tikta*	*Guru, Snigdha*	*Śīta*	*Madhura*
38.	*Tagara*	*Madhura, Katu, Tikta,, Kaṣāya*	*Sara, Laghu, Snigdha*	*Uṣṅa*	*Katu*
39.	*Tila (Kṛṣṇa)*	*Madhura, Tikta, Kaṣāya*	*Guru, Snigdha*	*Uṣṅa*	*Madhura*
40.	*Bhṛngarāja*	*Katu, Tikta*	*Rukṣa, Laghu*	*Uṣṅa*	*Katu*
41.	*Śāka*	*Kaṣāya*	*Laghu, Rukṣa*	*Śīta*	*Katu*
42.	*Tulasi*	*Katu, Tikta*	*Laghu, Rukṣa*	*Uṣṅa*	*Katu*
43.	*Anantā*	*Madhura, Tikta, Kaṣāya*	*Laghu, Rukṣa*	*Śīta*	*Katu*
44.	*Gokṣura*	*Madhura*	*Guru, Snigdha*	*Śīta*	*Madhura*
45.	*Plāndu*	*Madhura, Katu*	*Guru, Tikṣṇa Snigdha*	*Uṣṅa*	*Madhura*
46.	*Manjisthā*	*Kaṣāya, Tikta, Madhura*	*Guru, Rukṣa*	*Uṣṅa*	*Katu*
48.	*Kumāri*	*Tikta, Madhura*	*Guru, Snigdha,*	*Śīta*	*Katu*
49.	*Tilaka*	*Katu*	*Picchila*	*Uṣṅa*	*Katu*
50.	*Śālamalī*	*Madhura, Kaṣāya*	*Laghu, Snigdha, Picchila*	*Śīta*	*Madhura, Katu*
51.	*Tāramakṣica*	*Madhura, Tikta, Kaṣāya*	*Laghu*	*Sita*	*Madhura*
52.	*Pārada*	*Madhura, Amla, Lavaṇa, Katu, Kaṣāya*	*Guru, Sara, Snigdha*	*Uṣṅa*	*Madhura*
53.	*Gandhaka*	*Katu, Tikta*	*Laghu, Snigdha*	*Uṣṅa*	*Katu*
54.	*Haritāla*	*Katu, Kaṣāya*	*Laghu, Snigdha*	*Uṣṅa*	*Katu*
55.	*Hīraka*	*Śādraśa*	-	-	-
56.	*Viṣa*	*Madhura*	*Rukṣa, Tikṣṇa, Laghu, Vayavāyī, Vikāsī*	*Uṣṅa*	*Madhura*
57.	*Vidanga*	*Katu*	*Laghu, Rukṣa, Tikṣṇa*	*Uṣṅa*	*Katu*
58.	*Agnimantha*	*Tikta, Katu, Kaṣāya, Madhura*	*Rukṣa, Laghu*	*Uṣṅa*	*Katu*

Mode of Action of *Rasāyana* Drugs

The word "*Rasāyana*" addresses the "optimisation of circulating the nourishing foods through tissues & cells." So getting adequate quantity & quality of *Āhāra Rasa* with its proper circulation through channels is the main concept of *Rasāyana* Therapy. The concept of *Rasāyana* Therapy is not a single drug treatment but it is a comprehensive and specialized regimen capable of producing healthful longevity and improved mental faculties by acting at the level of *Rasa* (Nutrition), *Agni* (digestion & metabolism) and the *Srotāṁsi* (microcirculation), thus enabling the organism to procure the best qualities of different *Dhātus*. The *Rasāyana* Therapy is supposed to influence the very fundamental mechanisms of the living organism and to have rejuvenating effects on the body as well as the mind.

To evaluate the mode of action of *Rasāyana* one has to approach the whole process adopted in *Rasāyana* Therapy. In the process of *Rasāyana* Therapy factors involved can be considered as pre-requisite for *Rasāyana* Therapy which include—

Pūrva Karmās—*Snehana, Swedana*, *Samśodhana, Samsarjana* & devoidence of negative attitudes.

Pradhāna Karma—Finally consuming suitable *Rasāyana* Measure.

Therefore one has to include the efficacy of these *Pūrva Karmās* in the impact of *Rasāyana* Therapy. It may be pointed out that besides being of preparatory significance *Samśodhana Karmās* form a full therapy, is designed to eradicate the vitiated *Doṣās* and to maintain a state of normalcy and equilibrium which is the fundamental basis of health. Due to these procedures body tissues become free from residual materials, channels become clean, digestion and metabolism become adequate, ultimately leading to promotion of nutritional factors.

Most of the *Rasāyana* drugs (*Yoga/Kalpa*) have all the above fundamental qualities like stimulation of *Agni*, cleansing of *Srotāsa*, pacification of *Vāta Doṣa* required for achieving adequate *Āhāra Rasa*, along with the special quality of improving nutritional value of *Poṣaka Rasa* ultimately leading to the achievement of comprehensive effect as stated by *Ācārya Caraka* as "*Lābhopāyo Hi Śastānāma Rasādināma Rasāyanama* which produces the *Rasāyana* effects mentioned in terms of *Vayasthāpanā*, *Āyuṣkara*, *Medhākara* & *Urjaskara* etc.

Thus it is clear that *Rasāyana* drugs and measures act at one or all of the following three levels. As a result, rich, good and healthy *dhātus* are produced in the body—"*Lābhopāyo Hi Śastānāma Rasādināma Rasāyanama.*" This gives to a person longevity, vitality, lusture, improved intellect, immunity and happiness.

1. *Acting at the level of Rasa* by enriching the nutritional value of the circulating plasma e.g. *Śatāvari*, *Drākṣā*, *Śālparṇi* etc.

2. *Acting at the level of Agni* i.e. at the level of digestion & metabolism. This group of drugs improve the digestion, absorption and metabolism and have some anabolic effect e.g. *Pippalī*, *Harītakī*, *Citraka* etc.

3. *Acting at the level of Srotāmsi* i.e. at the micro-circulatory channels carrying nutrition to the tissues. These *Rasāyanās* cleanse and activate the microcirculatory channels—i.e. do *Sroto-Śudhi*. Thus tissue nourishment is improved considerably leading to improved tissue health and their quality e.g. *Guggulu*, *Pippalī*, *Rasona* etc.

The process of digestion converts the ingested food into *Āhāra Rasa* (the essence of food). This *Āhāra Rasa* gets into circulation to provide nourishment to various organs, tissues and finally to the individual cells-the unit of life. With the quality of circulation, adequate quality and quantity of *Āhāra Rasa*, adds an important dimension in order to ensure adequate nutrition to the substructures of physiology.

Literally the word "*Rasāyana*" addresses the optimisation of circulating the *nourishing* foods through tissues and cells. So getting adequate quantity and quality of *Āhāra Rasa* with its proper circulation through channels is the main concept of *Rasāyana*-Therapy. Such a phenomenon is considered conducive to the promotion of the qualities of *Dhātus* i.e. Tissue elements. The improved nutritional status and the better qualities of *Dhātus* lead to a series of secondary attributes of *Rasāyana* as longevity, immunity against diseases, improved mental and intellectual competence etc.

Considering the *Āyurvedic* concept of physiology the process in which formation of "*Āhāra Rasa*" and promotion of nutrition to imbue plumpness etc. of the body takes place through following modes.

Being stimulated by the *Jātharāgni, Agnis* specific to different *Manābhūtās* digest the various types of food articles producing thereby plumpness, strength, complexion, happiness as well as growth of the tissue elements of the entire body, where the process of metabolism goes on continuously like the passage of time and where all the *Dhātvāgnis, Vāta Doṣa* and *Srotāsa* (Channels of circulation) are unimpaired.[1]

---

१. विविधमशितं पीतं लीढं खादितं ... शरीरधातूनूर्जयति च।
धातवो हि धात्वाहारा: प्रकृतिमनुवर्तन्ते। (चरक सूत्र-२८/३)

Food articles are composed of five *Mahābhūtās*. *Agnis* specific to these five *Mahābhūtās* help in the digestion of their respective food ingredients.[1] But these *Bhūtagnis* start their work only when stimulated by *Jātharāgni*.[2] These are the two processes through which "*Āhāra Rasa*" formation takes place. To imbue plumpness etc. in the body, it is also necessary that the breakdown product of food articles should undergo metabolic transformation (*Pāka*) by *Dhātwāgnis* (or enzymes specific to each category of tissue elements). The process of metabolism goes on incessantly in the body by which there is continuous depletion of tissue elements which is replenished by the food and thus, the plumpness of the body is maintained.

In order that the promotion of plumpness of the body is maintained, along with *Dhātwāgni*, it is also necessary that the *Vāta Doṣa* (*Vyāna Vāyu*) which is the force for the transportation of nutrient material to various tissues and the channels of transport (circulation) should remain unimpaired.

Thus to maintain proper health of individuals the *Jātharāgni* (enzymes responsible for Gastro-intestinal digestion), *Bhūtāgni* (*Agnies* inherent in the five *Mahābhūtas* converting the heterogenous materials into homogenous ones), *Dhātwāgni* (Enzymes responsible for synthesis of tissue elements i.e. metabolic transformation), *Vyāna Vāyu* (Force of transformation of nutrient material) and *Srotasa* (Channels of transport) must be unimpaired.

This is where the concept of *Rasāyana* comes into picture. In true sense of the concept, *Rasāyana* therapy

---

१. भौमाप्याग्नेयवायव्या:...कृत्स्नश:। (चरक चिकित्सा-१५/१३-१४)

२. जाठरेणाग्निना...पचन्ति। इति। (चरक चिकित्सा-१५/१३ पर चक्रपाणि)

is not a single drug treatment, but is a comprehensive and specialised regimen capable of producing healthful longevity and improved mental faculties by acting at the level of *Rasa* (Nutrition), *Agni* (Digestion and metabolism) and the *Srotāmsi* (Microcirculation) thus enabling the organism to procure the best qualities of different *Dhātus*. The *Rasāyana* therapy is supposed to influence the very fundamental mechanisms of the living organism and to have rejuvenating effects on the body as well as the mind.

So as to evaluate the mode of action of *Rasāyana* one has to approach the whole process adopted in *Rasāyana* Therapy. In the process of *Rasāyana* Therapy factors involved are pre-requisites for *Rasāyana* i.e. (i) *Pūrva Karma,* which include—

1. *Snehana*
2. *Swedana*
3. *Samśodhana*
4. *Samsarjana*
5. Devoidance of negative attitudes

(ii) *Pradhāna Karma*

Finally consuming suitable *Rasāyana* measure.

Though *Rasāyana* Therapy is divided into two categories *Kutiprāveśika* & *Vātātapika* and it is mentioned that former has better efficacy.[1]

The emphasis of *Pūrva Karma* (Pre-requisite) implies on both the methods.

---

१. तयोः श्रेष्ठतरः पूर्वो विधिः स तु सुदुष्करः॥

(चरक चिकित्सा-१/४/२८)

Therefore one has to include the efficacy of these *Pūrva karma* in the impact of *Rasāyana* Therapy. It may be pointed out that besides being of preparatory significance *Samśodhana Karma* forms a full therapy which is designed to erradicate the vitiated *Doṣās* and to maintain a state of normalcy and equilibrium which is the fundamental basis of health.

Due to these procedures body tissues become free from residual material, channels become clear, digestion and metabolism become adequate ultimately leading to promotion of nutritional factors. Infact without consuming *Rasāyana* measures also one can attain the normalcy and equilibrium with purificatory procedures. So after going through these purificatory procedures it is quite obvious that the *Rasāyana* drugs act more vigourously. That is why the stress has been put forth on *Samśodhana* by *Ācāryās*.[1]

Ācārya Suśruta mentions *Samśodhana* as a preparatory procedure prior to *Rasāyana* & *Vājīkaraṅa* therapy.

Pancakarma not only eliminates the morbid humours *(Doṣās)* but it also removes the various types of obstruction ranging form the intra-cellular to the tissue, organ and system may be in the path of secretion, transportation, absorption & excretion. By regularizing all physiological systems in turn creates an ideal environment in the biological system, for the better bio-availability of the *Rasāyana* & *Vājīkaraṅa* drugs administered thereafter.

Thus it is clear that action of *Rasāyana* therapy works through whole process by acting at the levels of *Rasa* (Nutrition), *Agni* (Digestion & metabolism) and *Srotāmsi* (Microcirculation) enabling the organism to procure the best qualities of different *Dhātus*.

---

१. नाविशुद्धशरीरस्य युक्तो रसायनो विधिः।
न भाति वाससि म्लिष्टे रंगयोग इवाहितः।। (सुश्रुत चिकित्सा-२७/४)

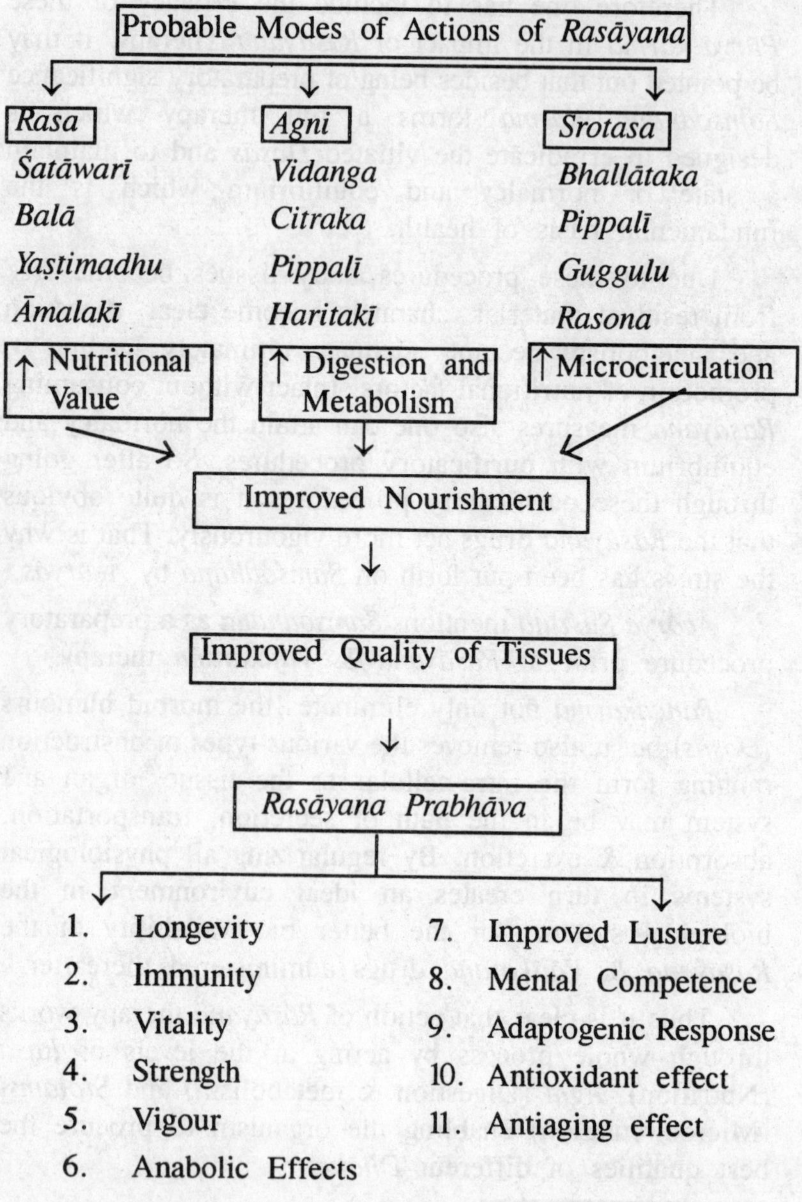
Probable Modes of Actions of Rasāyana
Rasa
Śatāwarī
Balā
Yaṣṭimadhu
Āmalakī
↑ Nutritional Value
Agni
Vidanga
Citraka
Pippalī
Haritakī
↑ Digestion and Metabolism
Srotasa
Bhallātaka
Pippalī
Guggulu
Rasona
↑Microcirculation
Improved Nourishment
Improved Quality of Tissues
Rasāyana Prabhāva
1. Longevity
2. Immunity
3. Vitality
4. Strength
5. Vigour
6. Anabolic Effects
7. Improved Lusture
8. Mental Competence
9. Adaptogenic Response
10. Antioxidant effect
11. Antiaging effect

Basic Physiology of *Rasāyana*

Āhāra → *Agni* → *Āhāra Rasa* → *Sapta Dhātu* Formation → *OJAS*

STEPS

1. *Pūrva Karma*

1. *Snehana* 2. *Swedana* 3. *Samśodhana* 4. *Samsarjana* 5. Devoidance of Negative Attitude	→	1. Cleanses *Srotasa* 2. Improves *Agni* 3. Maintains *Doṣic* Equilibrium 4. Makes way to improve Nutritional Quality of *Āhara Rasa*

2. *Pradhāna Karma*

1. Suitable *Rasāyana* Measure 2. *Kuti Prāveśika* (*kāmya*) 3. *Vātātapika* (1. *Naimittika*) (2. *Ājasrīka*) 4. According to *Vaya*, *Prakriti*, *Sātmya* etc.	→	1. Maintains unimpaired conditions of digestion, metabolism and micro circulation 2. Improves Quality of *Āhāra Rasa* 3. Provides adequate Nutrition to *Dhātus* 4. Stops/delays the phenomenon of disease and decay.

3. *Pascāta Karma*

Following of whole some Diet and Habits → Protects from Disease or Decay

4. Results To

1. Longevity
2. Strength
3. Vigour
4. Immunity
5. Vitality
6. Mental Competence

→ ***RASĀYANA PRABHĀVA***

Chapter IV

Biological Effects of *Rasāyana* Drugs

The concept of *Rasāyana* had invoked a good deal of scientific enthusiasm way back in late 60's. Few herbs have been explored for their specific biological effects on different dimension of health. Summarising these studies, there is clinching evidence on the multi-dimensional effects of herbs with *Rasāyana* attributes.

Anabolic Effects

Initial investigations on *Rasāyana* drugs were designed to elicit their role on metabolism and tissue building. Herbs like *Gambhāri* (Gmelina arborea) have shown a positive hint in this direction. Regular administration of such drugs was found to improve nitrogen balance and thus promote tissue building.

Anti Stress, Adaptogenic Effects

The process of living is subjected to many paradoxial situations. One of such a paradox is stress. To be precise, every living organism in this universe is positioned in some or other kind of stressful situation. It is practically difficult to define the normal or abnormal vlaues for stress and the quantum of it is highly variable. Over and above what matters the most is one's own threshold of tolerance. If you have a good tolerance, stress can do something really good for you. Therefore, we look at the means of improving our own tolerance and a *Rasāyana* drug could come to your rescue to some extent, perhaps.

Pharmacological investigations on drugs like *Aświagandhā* (Withania somnifera) and *Śilājatu* point to this unique biological effect of *Rasāyana* drugs. Accordingly a drug with *Rasāyana* quality can benefit the uses in two distinct ways. Firstly, it can neutralize the negative effects of stress on physiology and restore homeostasis.This effect is generally termed as Anti-stress effect. Secondly a long term administration of such drugs may enhance one's own tolerance levels and help to cope-up with stress better. This particular effect is termed as adaptogenic effect. In fact, the word "Adaptogenesis" found its place in the medical terminology only, after understanding some of these *Āyurvedic* drugs.

Immuno Modulatory Effect

Immunity (*Vyādhi kṣhmatva*) is another biological phenomenon with varied implications. At its first place, immune system works to fight back any kind of external invasions on the body e.g. on invasions by microbes. Immune system is a multilocational, multicomponent defence system guarding the body as a whole. Again, today's understanding goes immune system may also play a paradoxical role in the body. For example, when it works in a balanced manner it gaurds the body from invasions by microbes. When this defence system mechanism goes weak—the body suffers infections. You may need a drug, which can stimulate the immune cells to work more effectively.

On the contrary, immune system under selected circumstances may go berserk and can start doubting our own tissues and invade them ruthlessly. Such an abnormal phenomenon may lead to development of a class of disease entities called "Auto Immune Disorders." In such kind of complex problems, one may need to suppress the hyperacting immune complexes.

Rasāyana herbs are being continuously explored for their effects on immune system. Available evidences show that, these drugs can be used to modulate the immune functions. At one hand they may work to enhance immune functions and build you firm deep within, or they might pacify an angry immunity cell to be in its limits on the other. Thus a *Rasāyana* drug favours the host in both ways.

Nootropic Effects

Certainly, *Āyurveda* was fascinated with the idea of enhancing mental capabilities, and so we come across a specified term "*Medhya Rasāyana*." This term refers to a specified group of drugs which work upon the mind, the "*Medha*" some of these herbs were also investigated for their effect mainly on memory and learning abilities. *Brāhmi* (Bacopa monieri), *Śankhapuṣpī* (Convolvulus pluricaulis) etc. fall in this category. While these investigations testify the acclaimed effects to some extent, we may have to go a long way to understand their real role on memory and intelligence.

Prof. Bhattacharya (of IMS, BHU, Varanasi) worked extensively on the subject. And in his own words "*Medhya Rasāyana* may turn an idiot to a normal person but may not change a normal person to a genious." Thus he feels that those drugs are capable of improving mental faculties in abnormal situation to some extent but may not have a real promise for normal persons. But the reality remains, memory and intellect are not just confined to brain. If we realise precisely every cell has its own intellect. And no one knows the practical effect of *Medhya Rasāyana* drugs on this omnipresent cellular intellect—as of now.

Anti Oxidant Effect

Oxygen creates another paradoxical situation for a living cell to face with. There has been a tremendous understanding today on the rampaging effects of oxygen free radicals if generated in excess to the demand. Body takes care of these excess free radicals, by producing certain kinds of enzymes to some extent. When these natural mechanisms become inadequate, the concentration of free radicals go up in the tissues and lead to various diseases. Today, oxygen free radicals are implicated in a wide range of diseases starting from minor allergies to cancers.

Rasāyana drugs are now discovered to help the physiology in over coming such oxidative injury. Present understanding goes that a *Rasāyana* drug enhances the natural enzymatic defence mechanism of the body. While most of *Rasāyana* drugs exhibit antioxidant activity, they are likely to have some kind of tissue specificity.

This thought remains a hypothesis as of now and the specific site of action for each of the *Rasāyana* drugs is yet to be identified.

Anti Aging Effects

Administration of *Rasāyana* drugs appears to be associated with prevention of aging also. There have been only few investigations in this direction and they are too inadequate to prove or disprove ancient thoughts. Available evidences faintly indicated that *Rasāyana* drugs could influence the secretion of a hormone DHEA the deficiency of which is implicated in the process of aging. Neurotransmitter substance such as Norepinephrine, Acetyl Choline or Dopamine (Dopamine is also named as DHEA-Dihydroxy phenyl alanine) are released in stress conditions. Repeated stress on every cell causes aging process.

Rasāyana therapy is thus, associated with multidimensional effects on the physiology.

Chapter V

Āyurvedic Concepts of Aging (*Jarā*) and its Prevention with *Rasāyana*

The particular *Rasāyana* has to be selected for each individual appropriately in consideration of his *Vaya, Prakriti*, *Sātmya*, *Satva*, State of *Agni*, *Dhātus*, *Srotasa* & environmental factors like *Deṣa* & *Kāla* etc.

Ācārya Caraka has divided "*Vaya*" in three major parts[1]—

(i) *Bālyāwasthā* 1-30 yrs.

(ii) *Madhyamāwasthā* 31-60 yrs.

(iii) *Jīrṅāwasthā* 61-100 yrs.

Further *Bālyāwasthā* has been divided into two subparts—

(i) *Aparipakwadhātu Bālyāwasthā* 1-16 yrs.

(ii) *Viwardhamānadhātu Bālyāwastha* 17-30 yrs.

---

१. वयस्तश्चेति...वयोऽभिधीयते। तद्वयो यथा स्थूलभेदेन त्रिविधं-बालं, मध्यं, जीर्णमिति। (चरक विमान-८/१२२)

Ācārya Suśruta has divided '*Vaya*' in three major parts[1]—

(i) *Bāla* upto 16 yrs.

(ii) *Madhya* 17 to 70 yrs.

(iii) *Vṛdha* above 70 yrs.

Further *Bāla Awasthā* has been divided in three subparts—

(i) *Kṣīrapa* - upto 1 year

(ii) *Kṣīrannāda* - 1 to 2 years

(iii) *Annāda* - above 2 years

Madhya Awasthā has been divided in four subparts[2]—

(i) *Vṛdhi Awasthā* 17 to 20 yrs. of age

(ii) *Yowanāwasthā* 21 to 30 yrs. of age

(iii) *Sampurṅatā* 31 to 40 yrs. of age

(iv) *Parihāṅi Awasthā* 41 to 70 yrs. of age.

There is conventional understanding that *Rasāyana* therapy is a kind of Geriatric Care System and should be used in old age. This is not ture. *Rasāyana* is not only Geriatrics, but it is the science of nutrition i.e. *Poṣaṅa* and is applicable to all ages from Pediatrics to Geriatrics. Though its use may prolong life span and impart longevity the fundamental underlying theme of "*Rasāyana*" is

---

१. वयस्तु त्रिविधं-बाल्यं, मध्यं, वृद्धमिति।
तत्रोनषोडशवर्षीया बाला:। ते ....वृद्धमाचक्षते।।

(सुश्रुत सूत्र-३५/२९)

२. तस्य विकल्पो-वृद्धि:, यौवनं, संपूर्णता, परिहाणिरिति।

(सुश्रुत सुत्र-३५/२९)

"Nutrition" as is obvious from *Ācārya Caraka's* statement—"*Lābhopāyo Hi Śastānāma Rasādināma Rasāyana*ma".[1]

Nutrition is the primary attribute of *Rasāyana*, longevity and aging issues are one of its secondary attributes.

Ācārya Suśruta and *Vāgbhatta* have suggested that the optimum effect of *Rasāyana* Therapy can be obtained only if this therapy is used between 3rd & 5th decades of life "*Purve Vayasi Madhye wā*".[2]

The reason is simple, if there occur irreversible aging changes, the *Rasāyana* may not be that effective. Thus early adult and middle age is the best period for *Rasāyana* Therapy to have maximum of antiaging effects like *Vayasthāpanā*, *Āyuṣkara* & *Jarānāśana*.

This issue is described more elaborately by *Ācārya Śārangdhara* according to whom a person looses his 1. *Bālya*, 2. *Vṛddhi*, 3. *Chavi*, 4. *Medhā*, 5. *Twaka*, 6. *Dṛṣti*, 7. *Śukra*, 8. *Vikrama*, 9. *Buddhi* and 10.*Karmendṛya* in the 1st, 2nd, 3rd... upto 10th decades of life respectively. Thus specific *Rasāyana* drugs will have to be selected and administered in respective age groups.[3]

Healthful longevity has ever been the cherished desire of man. Man finds the real pleasure of life with full of activity and vigour during the period of youth. He hates old age. *Āyurveda* can tackle the health problems of the aged more efficiently because it has got one seperate branch termed as *Rasāyana Tantra* (Rejuvenation Therapy)

---

१. चरक चिकित्सा-१/१/७-८.

२. सुश्रुत चिकित्सा-२७/३

३. शार्ङ्गधर संहिता पूर्व खण्ड-६/१९.

which is mainly devoted for the promotion of both physical and mental health and prevention of *Jarā* (Aging) and disease.[1]

The *Āyurvedic* texts have also given due thought to the process of aging and related health problems. According to *Āyurveda*, the *Jarā* (Aging) is a natural phenomenon like hunger, thirst & sleep. *Āyurveda* divides whole span of life into 3 parts viz.—

(i) *Bālya* (Childhood)

(ii) *Madhya* (Young & Middle age)

(iii) *Vṛdha* (Old Age) The persons above 60 yrs. of age are considered as *Vṛdha*.[2]

Ācārya Suśruta has beautifully defined the old age by giving it a simile of decaying old house which may collapse during any rainy season.[3] By implication, it means that the declining tissues (*Dhātu*) of the aged persons are unable to tolerate the physical and mental stresses and strains, which earlier in childhood or young age might have passed without leaving any visible scar

---

१. रसायनं च तज्ज्ञेयं यज्जराव्याधिनाशनम्।
यथा अमृता सूदन्ती च गुग्गुलुश्च हरीतकी।।
(शार्ङ्गधर संहिता-४/१३-१४)

यज्जराव्याधिविध्वंसि वयस्तं भनकरं तथा।
चक्षुष्यं वृहणं वृष्यं भेषजं तद्रसायनम्।।
(भावप्रकाश पूर्व खण्ड-७३/१)

२. वयस्तश्चेति कालप्रमाण....बालं, मध्यं, जीर्णमिति।
(चरक विमान-८/१२२)

३. सर्वक्रियास्वसमर्थ जीर्णागारमिवाभिवृष्टमवसीदन्तं वृद्धमाचक्षते।।
(सुश्रुत सूत्र-३५/२९)

and in old age any such phenomenon may lead to serious illness or death. Therefore the aged persons require more attention and care particularly from the physicians so that they may remain physically and mentally sound during the last decades of their life.

Etymology of *Jarā*

The word *Jarā* is derived from "जॄष" *Dhātu*, which is meant for diminution of age.

"*Śabda Kalpa Druma*" States that the flaccidity of body tissue occuring due to age is called as *Jarā*.

Aetiology of *Jarā* (Aging)

Āyurveda categorises aetiological factors for any diseases as—

(i) *Swabhāvika*

(ii) *Āgantuka*

(iii) *Śarīrika*

(iv) *Mānasika*

Ācārya Suśruta has mentioned a group of naturally occuring diseases formed as *Swabhāva Bala Pravṛtta* which includes *Jarā* (Aging) also. *Ācārya Dalhaṅa* while commenting on the *Swabhāva Bala-Pravṛtta* mentions that this type of disease occurs due to the power of nature (*Prakṛti-Śakti Jāta*). According to *Ācārya Cakrapāṅi* the *Swabhāva* or nature of an individual depends upon the invisible factors hereditarily carried on by that particular race in which he is born.[1]

---

१. स्वभावो मानुषशरीरस्य जातिप्रतिबद्धोऽदृष्टकृतो भावः। इति।
(सुश्रुत सूत्र-२४/७ चक्रपाणि)

The word *Prakṛti* (Nature) here denotes to both the nature of a particular species and nature of an individual within the species. For instance, the onset of aging varies in different species and similarly within one species also the nature of an individual varies according to *Deśa* (Habitat), *Kāla* (time & environment), *Prakṛti* (temperament) and heredity and accordingly *Jarā* may appear early, timely or late with its less, moderate or more symptoms.

Ācārya Suśruta has divided the *Swabhāva Bala Pravṛtta* diseases in two groups[1] viz. *Kālaja* & *Akālaja*. In this way *Jarā* (Aging) is also divided into two groups viz.

1. *Kālaja Jarā*
2. *Akālaja Jarā*

I. *Kālaja Jarā* (Timely Aging)

The appearance of *Jarā* (aging) at the appropriate age i.e. above 60 years may be termed as *Kālaja Jarā*. This is considered accordingly to *Ācārya Caraka* but *Ācārya Suśruta* increases this limit to 70 years.[2] Actually speaking it is not a disease but the phenomenon which starts much earlier at about the age of 40 years. This type of *Jarā* is considered as *Parirakṣaṇa Kritta*,[3] because it occurs at its prescribed age or a bit late due to the carefully following the daily & seasonal schedules described in "*Swasthavṛtta*" and by performing the "*Śodhana*" at the proper time. Thus *Kālaja Jarā* is possible only if one

---

१. स्वभावबलप्रवृता ये क्षुत्पिपासाजरामृत्युनिद्राप्रभृतयः, तेऽपि द्विविधाः कालजाः, अकालजाश्च।

(सुश्रुत सूत्र-२४/७)

२. अत ऊर्ध्वमीषत्परिहाणियवित् सप्ततिरिति।

(सुश्रुत सूत्र-३५/२९)

३. तत्र परिरक्षणकृताः कालजाः, अपरिरक्षणकृता अकालजाः।

(सुश्रुत सूत्र-२४/७)

remains careful towards his health and therefore it may be a slow progressive and without disturbing much the physical health and mental faculties of aged.

II. *Akālaja Jarā* (Untimely Aging)

The appearance of signs and symptoms of *Jarā* (aging) before the age of 60/70 years may be described as *Akālaja Jarā*. This type of *Jarā* is considered as *Apari-Rakṣaṇa-kṛita*[1] because it occurs before the prescribed age for not taking the care of "*Swasthavṛtta*" (personal hygiene) and not getting the "*Śodhana*" (purification) done at the proper time as mentioned in *Āyurveda*.

According to *Ācārya Dalhaṅa* the main cause of *Akālaja Jarā* is one's carelessness towards his health.

By screening different *Āyurvedic* texts the hetus (aetiological factors) of *Akālaja Jarā* may be summarised as follows[2]—

---

१. तत्र परिरक्षणकृता: कालजा:, अपरिरक्षणकृता अकालजा:।

(सुश्रुत सूत्र-२४/७)

२. सर्वे शरीरदोषा भवन्ति ग्राम्याहारदम्ललवणकटुक्षार शुष्कशाकमांसतिल पलल पिष्टान्नभोजिनां...भगवान पुनर्वसुरात्रेय उवाच।

(चरक चिकित्सा-१/२/३)

अत्यध्वा विपरीतोऽस्माज्जरादौर्बल्य कृच्च स:।।

(सुश्रुत चिकित्सा-२४/७९)

पद्भ्यामतीव गमनेन तथाऽतिशीत-संसेवनेन च कदन्ननिषेवणाच्च।
वृद्धाङ्गनासततसंगमनाच्च चेतो दु:खादुदेति हि जरा समयाच्च नूनम्।।

(माधव निदान परिशिष्ट जरारोग निदानम्)

अध्वा जरा देहवतां पर्वतानां जलं जरा।
असम्भोगो जरा स्त्रीणां वाक्यशल्यं मनसो जरा।।

(म०भा०उ०प० ३९/७४)

यस्य भार्या वरुपाक्षी कश्मला कलह प्रिया।
उत्तरोत्तरवाद्रास्या सा जरा न जरा जरा।।
यस्य भार्याश्रितान्यत्र परमेश्माभिक्त्रंहिणी।
कृक्रियात्यक्तलज्जा च सा जरा न जरा जरा।।

(गरुड़ पुराण पूर्वखण्ड-३५/१०१)

Ahāraja Hetu

1. *Lavaṅa* (salt), *Amla* (sour), *Katu Rasa Pradhāna* (spicy food).
2. *Kṣāra* (Alkali)
3. *Śuṣka Śāka*, *Māmsa* (Dry Vegetables & meat)
4. *Tila Samyoga*
5. *Piṣṭhanna*
6. *Virudhanna* (Incompatible Diet)
7. *Asātmya anna* (Unfavourable Diet)
8. *Rukṣa anna* (Dry anna cereals)
9. *Abhiśyandy anna*
10. *Klinna, Guru anna* (Heavy *anna*)
11. *Puti, Paryuśita anna* (Polluted and Out dated).
12. *Viśamaśana* (Improper eating habits)
13. *Adhyaśana* (Over eating)

***Vihāraja Hetu*—**

1. *Atimārga gamana* (Excessive walk)
2. *Divā Swapna* (Day Sleeping)
3. *Nitya Strī Sevana* (Excessive intercourse)
4. *Nitya Madya Sevana* (Excessive intake of Alcohol)
5. *Viṣama Vyāyāma Sevana* (Improper exercise)
6. *Atimātrā Vyāyāma Sevana* (Excessive exercise)

***Mānasika* Hetu**

1. *Bhaya* (Fear)
2. *Krodha* (Anger)
3. *Śoka* (Sorrow)

4. *Lobha* (Greed)
5. *Moha* (Affection)
6. *Rukṣha Vāṅī* (Harsh Voice)

Other *Hetus*

1. *Kalaha Priya Bhāryā* (Quarrelsome wife)
2. *Kuputra* (Maladroit Son)

***Pūrva Rūpa* (Prodromal Signs) of *Jarā*[1]**

1. *Śakti Kṣīṅatā* (Loss of Power)
2. *Smriti Nāśa* (Loss of Memory)
3. *Glāni* (Detestation)
4. *Vali* (Wrinkles)
5. *Pālitya* (Greying of hair)
6. *Danta Śaithilyama* (Dental loosening)
7. *Swabhāva Viparyaya* (Change in nature)

---

१. क्षीणत्वमत्र समुदेति शरीरशक्तेरादौ क्रमेण तदनु स्मृतिनाश एव।
ग्लानिस्ततोऽप्यवयवेषु जनिर्बलीनां पालित्यमत्यधिकतो हि शिरोरुहेषु।।
दन्तस्य चापि शिथिलत्वमथ स्वभावे भूयान् विपर्यय इति प्रतिमानवं वै।
प्रायो जराऽऽगमनकालत एव पूर्वमव्यक्तमीक्ष्यत उपर्युदितं तु लक्ष्म।।
(माधवनिदान परिशिष्ट जरारोग निदानम्)

Rūpa* (Symptoms & Signs) of *Jarā

They are categorised as follows[1]—

Śarīrika Lakṣaṇās

1. *Vali* (Wrinkles in skin)
2. *Palita* (Greying of hair)
3. *Khālitya* (Alopecia)
4. *Danta Śaithilya* (Dental Lossening)
5. *Danta-Pāta* (Loss of teeth)
6. *Kṛśatā* (Emaciation)
7. *Hasta Pāda Kampa* (Tremors)
8. *Jihvā Kampa* (Tremor of tongue)
9. *Grivā Kampa* (Tremors of Neck)

---

१. अतः परं हीयमानधात्विन्द्रियबलंवीर्यपौरुषपराक्रमग्रहणधारणस्मरण वचन-विज्ञानभ्रश्यमानधातुगुणं वायुधातुप्रायं क्रमेण जीर्णमुच्यते आवर्षशतम्।

(चरक विमान-८/१२२)

अतो निमित्तं हि शिथिलीभवन्ति मांसानि, विमुच्यन्ते सन्धयः, विदह्यते रक्तं, विष्यन्दते चानल्पं मेदः, न सन्धीयतेऽस्थिषु मज्जा, शुक्रं न प्रवर्तत्ते, क्षयमुपैत्योजः, स एवं भूतो ग्लायति, सीदति निद्रातन्द्रालस्यसमन्वितो निरुत्साहः श्वसिति, असमर्थश्चेष्टानां शरीरमानसीनां नष्टस्मृत्ति बुद्धिच्छायो रोगाणामधिष्ठानभूतो न सर्वमायुरवाप्नोति।

(चरक चिकित्सा-१/२/३)

सप्ततेरुर्ध्वक्षीयमाणधात्विन्द्रियबलवीर्योत्साहमहन्यहनि वलीपलितखालित्य जुष्टं कासश्वासप्रभृतिभिरुपद्रवैरभिभूयमानं सर्वक्रियास्वसमर्थ।

(सुश्रुत सूत्र-३५/२९)

प्राग्रूप संकथितलक्ष्मचयप्रकाशो.......काल एव।।

(माधवनिदान परिशिष्टम् जरा रोग निदानम्)

10. *Namana* (Kyphosis)
11. *Śakti Kṣīṅatā* (Loss of Power)
12. *Balahāni* (Loss of energy)
13. *Vīrya Kṣaya* (Loss of semen)
14. *Puruṣārtha hāni* (Loss of vital power)
15. *Dhātu Kṣīṅatā* (Decay of tissues)
16.1 *Vāta Prakopa* (Aggravation of *Vāta*)
17. *Agnimāndya* (Loss of appetite)
18. *Vāta Vyādhī* (Neurological disorders)
19. *Śithilāngatā* (Looseness of body)
20. *Sandhimukti* (Dislocation of joints)
21. *Rakta Vidāha* (Burning sensation)
22. *Majjā Kṣīṅatā* (Decay of Bone Marrow)
23. *Śukra Aparvartana* (Azoospermia)
24. *Oja Kṣaya* (Loss of immunity)

Mānasika Lakśaṅās

1. *Gāmbhirya* (Seriousness)
2. *Avasannātā* (Silence)
3. Loss of *Ekāgratā* (Concentration)
4. *Smriti Nāśa* (Loss of memory)
5. *Ekānta priyatā* (Loneliness)
6. *Glāni* (Detestation)
7. *Nairaśya* (Depression)
8. *Swabhāva Parivartana* (Change of Nature)
9. *Cintā* (Anxiety)
10. *Krodha* (Anger)
11. *Dhṛti Nāśa* (Loss of retention power)

12. *Utsāha Kṣīṅatā* (Loss of energy)
13. *Ghṛṅā* (To hate)

Viśeṣa Lakshaṅās

1. *Driṣti Māndya* (Diminition of vision)
2. *Śravaṅa Śakti Alpatā* (Diminition of hearing)
3. *Vāka Śakti Hāni* (Diminition of speech)

Probable Effects on Various *Srotasa* Due to *Jarā* (Aging)

1. *Prāṅa Vaha Srotasa* - *Swāskṛchratā* (Dyspnoea)
2. *Udaka Vaha Srotasa* - *Niṣthivana* (Expectoration)
3. *Anna Vaha Srotasa* - *Agnimāndya*, *Aruci* (Loss of appetite, Anorexia)
4. *Rasa Vaha Srotasa* - *Twaka Śaithilya*, *Vali*, *Rukṣatā*, *Pāndu* (Anaemia) *Palita* (Greying of hair)
5. *Rakta Vaha Srotasa* - *Śaityatā*, *Raktapitta* (Bleeding tendency), *Dhamani kāthinya* (Atherosclerosis), *Raktālpatā* (Anaemia)
6. *Māmsa Vaha Srotasa* - *Māmsa Śaithilya*, *Kārśya* (Weight loss), *Arbuda* (Cancers-Tumours)
7. *Medo Vaha Srotasa* - *Rūkṣata*, *Kārśyata* (Cachexia), *Prameha* (Diabetes Mellitus & other urinary diseases)

8. *Asthi Vaha Srotasa*	-	*Asthibhanguratā / Asthi suśiratā* (Osteoporosis), *Dantakṣaya, Sandhijādyatā, Sandhimuktatā* (Dislocation of joints), *Sandhivāta* (Osteo arthritis)
9. *Majjā Vaha Srotasa*	-	*Asthisuśirata* (Osteoporosis) *Bhrama* (Vertigo)
10. *Śukra Vaha Srotasa*	-	*Śukrālpatā* (Oligospermia), *Jarājanya Klaibya* (Impotency)
11. *Mutra Vaha Srotasa*	-	*Mutrādhikya* (Polyurea), *Aṣthilā* (Prostate enlargement)
12. *Puriṣa Vaha Srotasa*	-	*Vibandha* (Constipation), *Vātasancaya* (Flatulence), *Ādhmāna, Ātopa.*
13. *Mano Vaha Srotasa*	-	*Smritināśa* (Loss of memory) *Nairāśya* (Depression) *Ekānta priyatā* (Loneliness) etc.

Process of Aging in Different Body Tissues

The question may arise whether the aging starts simultaneously in all the tissues and organs or it affects them at the different years of age. The close perusal of the available literature reveals that "*Aśṭānga Samgraha*" is the first treatise, which has thrown some light on this problem. It has been mentioned that one particular thing is being lost after passing the each decade of life. After passing the first decade of life, the childhood also passes, after the second decade the growth stops, after the third decade *prabhā* (complexion) vanishes, after the fourth decade *medhā* (intellect) starts declining and at the end of the fifth decade the *Varṅa/Kānti* (lusture) is lost. Similarly at the end of sixth, seventh, eighth, ninth and tenth decades of life *Śukra* (semen including sperms), *Akśi* (vision), *Śruti* (hearing), *Mana* (mind) and functions of remaining special senses and motor organs are lost respectively.[1]

Ācārya Śārangadhara has divided the 120 years span of life into 12 decades,[2] and decade wise loss accordingly to him has been shown in the following table. *Ācārya Bhāvaprakāśa* has also expressed similar views.[3]

---

१. बाल्येवृद्धि प्रभा मेधांत्वक्शुक्राक्षीश्रुतीन्द्रियम्।
दशकेषु क्रमाद्यान्ति मनस्सर्वेन्द्रियाणि च।।
(अष्टाङ्ग संग्रह शारीर-८/२५)

२. बाल्यं वृद्धिश्छविर्मेधा त्वग्दृष्टिः शुक्रविक्रमौ।
बुद्धिः कर्मेन्द्रियं चेतो जीवितं दशतो ह्रसेत।।
(शार्ङ्गधर संहिता पूर्वखण्ड-६/२०)

३. बाल्यंवृद्धिश्छविर्मेधात्वग्दृष्टि शुक्र विक्रमौ।
बुद्धिः कर्मेन्द्रियः चेतो जीवितं दशतो ह्रसेत।।
(भाव प्रकाश ४/५०)

Table Showing Tissues and Mental Faculties Affected by Aging During Various Decades of Life.

Decade	*Aśṭānga Samgraha*	*Śāranga-dhara*	*Bhāvaprakāśa*
I	Childhood	Childhood	Childhood
II	Growth	Growth	Growth
III	*Prabhā* (Body Glow)	*Prabhā*	*Prabhā*
IV	*Medhā* (Intellect)	*Medhā*	*Medhā*
V	*Varṅa* (Lusture)	*Varṅa*	*Varṅa*
VI	*Śukra* (Semen)	Vision	Vision
VII	Vision	*Śukra*	*Śukra*
VIII	Hearing	*Vikrama* (Valour)	*Vikrama*
IX	Mind	*Buddhi*	*Buddhi*
X	Remaining Senses	Motor Organs	Motor Organs
XI	———	Mind	Mind
XII	———	Life	Life

It is obvious from the foregoing that aging is a slow and continuous process which affects various bodily tissues at different times. Some may doubt whether *Prabhā* or *Chavi* (body glow) is to be included in aging process but there may not be two opinions regarding the inclusion of declining in *Medhā* (intellect), the part of aging. In this way the process of aging according to *Āyurveda* definitely begins in the fourth decade of life. There after the process enhances and it affects one by one the functions of vital tissues and special senses like vision, *Śukra*, hearing etc.

Management of *Jarā* (Aging) with *Rasāyana*

First of all the question arises whether the aging process is reversible or not? And if it is reversible then how to achieve it? In this regard the following facts mentioned in *Āyurveda* may be taken into consideration.

As mentioned earlier *Jarā* (aging) and death are *Swabhāvika* (Natural) phenomenon and *Ācārya Caraka* considers them as *Swabhava Niśpratikṛyāha.*[1] i.e. by nature these are incurable. But in another context, while describing the best *Bhāva* (Things/*Agrya Sangraha*) for the various medical problems, *Ācārya Caraka* mentions "*Jarā yapyanama*" which means *Jarā* (aging) is on the top amongst the diseases which can not be cured but the patient may be kept symptoms free by proper treatment. *Ācārya Cakrapāṅi* while commenting on the word "*Niśpratikṛya*" mentions that ordinary treatment has got no effect on aging, but *Rasāyana* Therapy (specially *Kutiprāveśika Rasāyana*) is effective against it.[2] It has been clearly mentioned in *Caraka Samhitā* that old *Cyavana Ṛṣī* became younger after the use of *Rasāyana* Therapy.[3]

---

१. कालस्य परिणामेन जरामृत्युनिमित्तजा:।
रोगा: स्वभाविका दृष्टा: स्वभावो निष्प्रितिक्रिया।।
(चरक शारीर-१/११५ चक्रपाणि)

२. निष्प्रतिक्रिय इति साधारण चिकित्सा रसायनवर्ज्यया न।
प्रतिक्रियते रसायनेन तु प्रतिक्रियत एव।।
(चरक शारीर-१/११५ चक्रपाणि)

३. भार्गवश्चच्यवन: कामी वृद्ध: सन् विकृति गत:।
वीतवर्णस्वरोपेत: कृतस्ताभ्यां पुनर्युवा।
(चरक चिकित्सा-१/४/४४)

Similarly in *Vedic* literature references of Rejuvenation of *Ṛṣī Vandan* is[1] found. In this way the premature aging can be treated successfully by the *Rasāyana* therapy. However, *Rasāyana* is also not a complete cure of the *Jarā* as it can just check or delay the aging process for some time and as soon as the effect of *Rasāyana* vanishes, the process of aging starts again leading to the end of life.

As mentioned earlier *Ācārya Dalhaṅa* is of the view that *Akālaja Jarā* can easily be cured while *Kālaja Jarā* requires continuous care with *Rasāyana* drugs i.e. it is of "*Yāpya*" type.[2]

On the basis of foregoing it can be said that the aging can be checked and retracted to some extent by the timely and proper use of *Āyurvedic* principles of daily and seasonal schedules. *Rasāyana* Therapy is effective for both *Kālaja* and *Akālaja* types of *Jarā* by means of treating *Akālaja Jarā* and retarding the *Kālaja Jarā* maintains the physical and mental health of the aged, so that they may remain relevant to the society even in their last decades of life.

Ways to Combat Aging

Newer discipline of modern medicine states that aging occurs due to malfunction of DNA—repair mechanism and if it could be reversed it would slow down the process of aging. Aging, like cancer and so many genetic neuro-

---

१. ऋग्वेद-१/११९/७

२. अतएवं कालकृतानां नोपचारोऽस्ति, याप्यतैवास्ति भोजनपानरसायनां दिभि:, ... तस्मिन ये भवन्ति ते अकालकृता: तेषां च यथादोषं यथारोगं च प्रतीकार:।। (सुश्रुत सूत्र-२४/७ डल्हण।)

logical disorders, occurs due to DNA damage. Genetical damage occurs due to alterations in its structure, breaking of its strands. Though damage to DNA in the body is a continuous process, the cells keep them repairing. But Aging retards such a capacity. The accumulated DNA damage results in wrong kinds of signals and wrong proteins being synthesised, when the proteins do not function properly the cell dies.

The repair of the DNA involves many enzymes & proteins. The defect lies in the DNA polymerase (beta) molecules which carries out synthesis of the patch to be repaired. The dysfunction of this enzyme causes aging in the brain neurons. Some how correction of this defect may give chance that DNA repair capacity can be resurrected in aging neuron. These processes are still in experimental stages but another theory of aging is the free radical theory. Free radicals may also damage DNA. There are evidences that various exogenous & endogenous antioxidants are capable of inhibiting free radical formation.

So antioxidant therapy seems to be very important preventive measure in order to lessens tissue damage and the genetic damage also. These antioxidants help in maintainging the balance between the ROS generation and its eradication.

One of the contributing factors to the decline of cognitive function is the damaging effect of free radicals exposure. Free radicals are atoms or group of atoms that can cause damage to cells by a process called oxidation, which impairs the immune system and leads to infection and degenerative diseases. Environmental pollution, radiation, processed food and smoke are significant contributors to the release of free radicals. They are also produced in human body through sun exposure and stress. Antioxidants play a major role to retard this process. Vitamin A, C, E, B-complex are well established antioxidants.

The propable mode of action of *Rasāyana* drugs could be through chelation of free radicals (ferrous ions) and also as a chain breaker. It has been reported by scientific studies that *Rasāyana* drugs are potent antioxidant drugs.

Chapter VI

Rasāyana Described in *Caraka Samhitā*

First Chapter of *Cikitsā Sthāna* of *Caraka Samhitā*, namely "*Rasāyana Adhyāya*" is subdivided into four "*Pādās*" (Sub-chapters), which are—

1. *Abhayāmalakīya Rasāyana Pāda*
2. *Prāṅakāmīya Rasāyana Pāda*
3. *Kara Pracitiya Rasāyana Pāda*
4. *Āyurveda Samutthānīya Rasāyana Pāda*

Following *Rasāyanās* are described in these four *Rasāyana Pādās* (Sub-chapters)—

1. In First *Rasāyana Pāda*

1. *Brāhma Rasāyana* (first)
2. *Brāhma Rasāyana* (second)
3. *Cayavana Prāśa Rasāyana*
4. *Āmalaka Rasāyana*
5. *Harītakyādi Yoga* (first)
6. *Haritakyādi Yoga* (second)

Total 6 *Rasāyana Yogās*

2. In Second *Rasāyana Pāda*

1. *Śatapāka Āmalaka Ghṛta*

2. *Sahastrapāka Āmalaka Ghṛta*
3. *Āmalkāvaleha* (first)
4. *Āmalaka Cūrṇa*
5. *Vidangāvleha*
6. *Āmalkāvaleha* (second)
7. *Nāgabalā Rasāyana*
8. *Balā Rasāyana*
9. *Atibalā Rasāyana*
10. *Candana Rasāyana*
11. *Agru Rasāyana*
12. *Dhava Rasāyana*
13. *Tiniśa Rasāyana*
14. *Khadira Rasāyana*
15. *Śinśapā Rasāyana*
16. *Asana Rasāyana*
17. *Amṛtā Rasāyana*
20. *Muktā Rasāyana*
21. *Śveta Rasāyana*
22. *Jīwantī Rasāyana*
23. *Atirasā Rasāyana*
24. *Mandūkaparṅī Rasāyana*
25. *Sthīrā Rasāyana*
26. *Punarnavā Rasāyana*
27. *Bhallātaka Kṣīra*
28. *Bhallātaka Kṣodra*
29. *Bhallātaka Taila*
30. *Bhallātaka Guḍa*

31. *Bhallātaka Yūṣa*
32. *Bhallātaka Sarpī*
33. *Bhallātaka Palala*
34. *Bhallātaka Sattū*
35. *Bhallātaka Lavaṅa*
36. *Bhallātaka Tarpaṅa*

Total 36 Rasāyana Yogās

3. In Third *Rasāyana Pāda*

1. *Āmlkāyasa Brāhma Rasāyana*
2. *Kewalāmalaka Rasāyana*
3. *Lauhādi Rasāyana*
4. *Endra Rasāyana*
5. *Mandūkaparṅī Medhya Rasāyana*
6. *Yaṣṭimadhu Medhya Rasāyana*
7. *Guducī Medhya Rasāyana*
8. *Śankhapuṣpi Medhya Rasāyana*
9. *Pippalī Rasāyana* (First)
10. *Pippalī Rasāyana* (Second)
11. *Pippalī Vardhamāna Rasāyana*
12. *Triphalā Rasāyana* (First)
13. *Triphalā Rasāyana* (Second)
14. *Triphalā Rasāyana* (Third)
15. *Triphalā Rasāyana* (Fourth)
16. *Śilājatu Rasāyana*

Total 16 Rasāyana Yoga

4. In Fourth *Rasāyana Pāda*

1. *Indrokta Rasāyana* (First)
2. *Droṅi Prāveśika Rasāyana*

3. *Indrokta* **Rasāyana** (second)
4. *Ācāra Rasāyana*

Total 4 *Rasāyana Yoga*.

In reference to "*Divya Rasāyana Ausdhi*" *Mahṛṣi Ātreya* has described nine following medicines.[1] *Cakrapāṅi* has clearly indicated that these *Rasāyana-auṣadhis* are rare, & their existence today is doubtful.[2]

Ācārya Caraka has described 10 *Jīvanīya Dravya* having *Rasāyana* **Prabhāva**.[3] These include—

1. *Jīvaka*
2. *Ṛṣabhaka*
3. *Medā*
4. *Mahāmedā*
5. *Kākolī*
6. *Kṣīrakākolī*
7. *Mudagaparṅī*
8. *Māṣaparṅī*
9. *Jīwantī*
10. *Madhuka* **(Mulethī)**

---

१. ब्रह्म सुवर्चला नामौषधिर्या हिरण्य क्षीरा, पुष्कर सदृश पत्रा, आदित्य पर्णी नामौषधिर्या 'सूर्यकान्ता' इति विज्ञायते सुर्वण क्षीरा सूर्य मण्डलाकारपुष्पा च नारीनामौषधि... ... ... सहस्त्राण्यायुरनुपद्रवं चेति।
(चरक चिकित्सा-१/४/७)

२. ब्रह्म सुवर्चला प्रभृतयो यथोक्त लक्षणा दिव्यौषधयो नाति प्रसिद्धा।
(चरक चिकित्सा-१/४/७, चक्रपाणि)

३. जीवकर्षभकौ मेदा महामेदा काकोली क्षीर काकोली मुदगपर्णी माषपर्णी जीवन्ती मधुकमिति दशेमानि जीवनीयानि भवन्ति। (चरकसूत्र-४/११)

Single *Rasāyana* Drugs Described in *Caraka Samhitā*

SN.	*Rasāyana Dravya*	Reference
1.	*Harītakī*	*Ca.Ci. 1/1/25*
2.	*Āmalakī*	*Ca.Ci. 1/2/8*
3.	*Śankhapuṣpī*	*Ca.Ci. 1/3/30-31*
4.	*Mandūkaparṅī*	*Ca.Ci. 1/3/30-31*
5.	*Madhuyaṣṭī*	*Ca.Ci. 1/3/30-31*
6.	*Guducī*	*Ca.Ci. 1/3/30-31*
7.	*Pippalī*	*Ca.Ci. 1/3/32-35*
8.	*Śilājatu*	*Ca.Ci. 1/3/48-65*
9.	*Kākamacī*	*Ca.Su. 27/90*
10.	*Vidārīkanda*	*Ca.Su. 27/120*
11.	*Bhallātaka*	*Ca.Ci. 1/2/13-22*
12.	*Balā*	*Ca.Ci. 1/2/12*
13.	*Atibalā*	*Ca.Ci. 1/2/12*
14.	*Śveta Candana*	*Ca.Ci. 1/2/12*
15.	*Kṛṣṅa Agara*	*Ca.Ci. 1/2/12*
16.	*Dhava*	*Ca.Ci. 1/2/12*
17.	*Tiniśa*	*Ca.Ci. 1/2/12*
18.	*Khadira*	*Ca.Ci. 1/2/12*
19.	*Śīsama*	*Ca.Ci. 1/2/12*
20.	*Asana (Vijayasāra)*	*Ca.Ci. 1/2/12*
21.	*Jiwantī*	*Ca.Ci. 1/2/12*
22.	*Muktā (Rāsnā)*	*Ca.Ci. 1/2/12*
23.	*Śweta (Aprājitā)*	*Ca.Ci. 1/2/12*
24.	*Ati Rasā*	*Ca.Ci. 1/2/12*
25.	*Sthīrā (Sariwana)*	*Ca.Ci. 1/2/12*
26.	*Punarnavā*	*Ca.Ci. 1/2/12*
27.	*Guggulū*	*Ca.Ci. 28/241*
28.	*Nāgabalā*	*Ca.Ci. 1/2/11*
29.	*Kṣīra*	*Ca.Su. 25/38*
30.	*Ghṛta*	*Ca.Su. 25/38*
31.	*Pippalī Vardhamāna Rasāyana*	*Ca.Ci. 1/3/36-40*

Note : *Ca.* = *Caraka*
Ci. = *Cikitsā*
Su. = *Sūtra*

Rasāyana Yoga Described in _Caraka Samhitā_

SN.	*Rasāyana Yoga*	Reference
1.	*Brahma Rasāyana*	*Ca.Ci. 1/1/38-57*
2.	*Braham Rasāyana* (second)	*Ca.Ci. 1/1/58*
3.	*Cayavana Prāśa*	*Ca.Ci. 1/1/62-74*
4.	*Āmalaka Rasāyana* (fourth)	*Ca.Ci. 1/1/75*
5.	*Haritakyādi Rasāyana*	*Ca.Ci. 1/1/76*
6.	*Haritakyādi Yoga*	*Ca.Ci. 1/1/77*
7.	*Āmalaka Ghṛta*	*Ca.Ci. 1/2/4*
8.	*Āamalakāvleha*	*Ca.Ci. 1/2/7*
9.	*Āmalaka Cūrṅa*	*Ca.Ci. 1/2/8*
10.	*Vidangāvleha*	*Ca.Ci. 1/2/9*
11.	*Āmalakāvaleha*	*Ca.Ci. 1/2/10*
12.	*Āmalakāyasa Brahma Rasāyana*	*Ca.Ci. 1/3/3-6*
13.	*Lauhādi Rasāyana*	*Ca.Ci. 1/3/15-23*
14.	*Endra Rasāyana*	*Ca.Ci. 1/3/24-29*
15.	*Pippalī Rasāyana*	*Ca.Ci. 1/3/32-35*
16.	*Triphalā Rasāyana* (first)	*Ca.Ci. 1/3/41-42*
17.	*Triphalā Rasāyana* (second)	*Ca.Ci. 1/3/43-44*
18.	*Triphalā Rasāyana* (third)	*Ca.Ci. 1/3/45*
19.	*Triphalā Rasāyana* (fourth)	*Ca.Ci. 1/3/46-47*
20.	*Indrokta Rasāyana*	*Ca.Ci. 1/4/6*
21.	*Droṅī Prāveṣika Rasāyana*	*Ca.Ci. 1/4/7*

22.	*Indrokta Rasāyana* (Second)	*Ca.Ci. 1/4/16-26*
23.	*Brāhmī Ghṛta*	*Ca.Ci. 10/25*
24.	*Pancagavya Ghṛta*	*Ca.Ci. 10/17*
25.	*Mahā Pancagavya Ghṛta*	*Ca.Ci. 10/18-24*
26.	*Agastya Harītakī*	*Ca.Ci. 18/57-62*
27.	*Śatapāka-Sahastra Pāka Balā Taila*	*Ca.Ci. 29/119-120*
28.	*Kṣīra Sarpivṛṣya Yoga*	*Ca.Ci. 50/203*
29.	*Yāpana Vasti*	*Ca.Si. 12/2*
30.	*Niruha Vasti*	*Ca.Ci. 30/149-150*
31.	*Mustādi Yāpnā Vasti*	*Ca.Si. 12/15 (1)*
32.	*Balādi Yāpnā Vasti*	*Ca.Si. 12/15 (5)*
33.	*Balavardhaka Vasti*	*Ca.Si. 12/17 (1)*
34.	*Yogarāja*	*Ca.Ci. 16/81-87*

Note : *Ca. = Caraka*
Su. = Sūtra
Ci. = Cikitsā
Si. = Siddhi

Rasāyana* Therapy Indicated in Various Disorders in *Caraka Samhitā

SN.	Disorders	*Rasāyana* Used	Reference
1.	*Jwara*	*Catuha Snehā-nuvāsana Vasti*	*Ca.Si. 12/1*
	Jwara	*Balādi Yāpnā Vasti*	*Ca.Si. 12/15 (5)*
	Viṣama Jwara	*Mustādi Yāpnā Vasti*	*Ca.Si. 12/15(1)*
	Viṣama Jwara	*Agastya Harītakī*	*Ca.Ci. 18/57-62*
	Viṣama Jwara	*Pippalī Rasāyana*	*Ca.Ci.1/3/32-35*
	Viṣama Jwara	*Yogarāja*	*Ca.Ci. 16/81-87*
	Viṣama Jwara	*Harītakī*	*Ca-Si. 1/29-34*
	Jwara	*Pancagavya Ghṛta*	*Ca.Si. 10/7*
2.	*Rakta Pitta*	*Goghṛtādi Vasti*	*Ca.Si. 12/12*
	Pittaja Vyādhi	*Madhu Ghṛtādi Vasti*	*Ca.Si. 12/14*
	Rakta Vikāra	*Mustādi Yāpnā Vasti*	*Ca.Si. 12/15(1)*
3.	*Gulma*	*Mādhawādi Vasti*	*Ca.Si. 12/13*
	Gulma	*Balādi Yāpana Vasti*	*Ca.Si. 12/15*
	Gulma	*Mahā Pancagavya Ghṛta*	*Ca.Ci. 10/18-24*
	Gulma	*Pippalī Rasāyana*	*Ca.Ci. 1/3/32-35*
	Gulma	*Harītakī*	*Ca.Ci. 1/29-34*
	Rakta Gulma	*Catuha Sneha-Anuvāsana Vasti*	*Ca.Si. 12/1*
4.	*Prameha*	*Madhwādi Vasti*	*Ca.Si. 12/13*
	Prameha	*Yogarāj*	*Ca.Ci. 6/81-87*
	Prameha	*Harītakī*	*Ca.Ci. 1/29-34*
5.	*Kuṣṭha*	*Madhwādi Vasti*	*Ca.Si. 12/13*
	Kuṣṭha	*Endra Rasāyana*	*Ca.Ci.1/3/24-29*
	Kuṣṭha	*Śilājatu*	*Ca.Ci. 7/71-72*
	Kuṣṭha	*Harītakī*	*Ca.Ci. 1/29-34*

6.	*Rājayakṣmā*	*Harītakī*	*Ca.Ci. 1/29-34*
	Rājayakṣmā	*Yogarāj*	*Ca.Ci. 16/81-87*
	Rājayakṣmā	*Pippalī Rasāyana*	*Ca.Ci. 1/3/32-35*
	Ụrogata Roga	*Cayavanaprāśa*	*Ca.Ci. 1/1/62-74*
7.	*Unmāda*	*Mustādi Yāpnā Vasti*	*Ca.Ci. 12/15(1)*
	Unmāda	*Mahā Pancagavya Ghṛta*	*Ca.Ci. 10/18-24*
	Unmāda	*Bṛāhmi Ghṛta*	*Ca.Ci. 10/25*
8.	*Apasmāra*	*Mahāpancagavya Ghṛta*	*Ca.Ci. 10/18-24*
	Apasmāra	*Pancagavya Ghṛta*	*Ca.Ci. 10/17*
	Apasmāra	*Brāhmī Ghṛta*	*Ca.Ci. 10/25*
	Apasmāra	*Yogarāja*	*Ca.Ci. 16/81-87*
9.	*Kṣatakṣīṇa*	*Yamaka Anuvāsana Vasti*	*Ca.Ci. 12/18(3)*
	Kṣatakṣīṇa	*Catuha Sneha-Anuvāsana Vasti*	*Ca.Ci. 12/18(1)*
	Kṣatakṣīṇa	*Mustādi Yāpnā Vasti*	*Ca.Si. 12/15(1)*
10.	*Śvathū (Śotha)*	*Mahā Pancagavya Ghṛta*	*Ca.Ci. 10/18-24*
	Śvathū	*Pippali Rasāyana*	*Ca.Ci. 1/3/32-35*
	Śvathū	*Harītakī*	*Ca.Ci. 1/29-34*
	Śvathū	*Śilājatu*	*Ca.Ci. 12/49*
	Śvathū	*kansa Harītakī*	*Ca.Ci. 12/50-52*
11.	*Udara Roga*	*Mahā Pancagavya Ghṛta*	*Ca.Ci. 10/18-24*
	Udara Roga	*Endra Rasāyana*	*Ca.Ci. 1/3/24-29*
	Udara Roga	*Harītakī*	*Ca.Ci. 1/29-34*
12.	*Arśa Roga*	*Madhwādi Vasti*	*Ca.Si. 12/13*
	Arśa Roga	*Mustādi Yāpnā Vasti*	*Ca.Ci. 12/15(1)*
	Arśa Roga	*Agastya Harītakī*	*Ca.Ci. 18/57-62*
	Arśa Roga	*Mahā Pancagavya Ghṛta*	*Ca.Ci. 10/18-24*

Arśa Roga		*Yogarāja*	*Ca.Ci. 16/81-87*
	Arśa Roga	*Harītakī*	*Ca.Ci. 1/29-34*
13.	*Grahaṇī*	*Agastya Harītakī*	*Ca.Ci. 18/57-62*
	Grahaṇī	*Pippalī Rasāyana*	*Ca.Ci. 1/3/32-35*
	Grahaṇī	*Harītakī*	*Ca.Ci. 1/29-34*
14.	*Pāndū*	*Mahā Pancagavya Ghṛta*	*Ca.Ci. 10/18-24*
	Pāndū	*Yogarāj*	*Ca.Ci. 16/81-87*
	Pāndū	*Pippalī Rasāyana*	*Ca.Ci. 1/3/32-35*
	Pāndū	*Śilājatu Vataka*	*Ca.Ci. 16/87-92*
	Pāndū	*Harītakī*	*Ca.Ci. 1/29-34*
15.	*Kāmalā*	*Yogarāja*	*Ca.Ci. 16/81-87*
	Kāmalā	*Mahā Pancagavya Ghṛta*	*Ca.Ci. 10/18-24*
	Kāmalā	*Pancagavya Ghṛta*	*Ca.Ci. 10/17*
	Kāmalā	*Harītakī*	*Ca.Ci. 1/29-34*
16.	*Halimaka*	*Mahā Pancagavya Ghṛta*	*Ca.Ci. 10/18-24*
17.	*Hikkā*	*Agastya Harītakī*	*Ca.Ci. 16/57-62*
	Hikkā	*Pippalī Rasāyana*	*Ca.Ci. 1/32-35*
18.	*Śwāsa*	*Yogarāja*	*Ca.Ci. 16/81-87*
	Śwāsa	*Yamaka Anuvāsana Vasti*	*Ca.Si. 12/18(3)*
	Śwāsa	*Agastya Harītakī*	*Ca.Ci. 18/57-62*
	Śwāsa	*Pippalī Rasāyana*	*Ca.Ci. 1/1/32-35*
19.	*Tamaka Śwāsa*	*Cayavanaprāśa*	*Ca.Ci. 1/1/62-74*
	Tamaka Śwāsa	*Harītakī*	*Ca.Ci. 1/29-34*
20.	*Kāsa*	*Yogarāja*	*Ca.Ci. 16/81-87*
	Kāsa	*Yamaka Anuvāsana Vasti*	*Ca.Si. 12/18(3)*
	Kāsa	*Balādi Yāpnā Vasti*	*Ca.Si. 12/15(5)*
	Kāsa	*Mustādi Yāpnā Vasti*	*Ca.Si. 12/15(1)*
	Kāsa	*Agastya Harītakī*	*Ca.Ci. 18/57-62*
	Kāsa	*Pippalī Rasāyana*	*Ca.Ci. 1/3/32-35*

	Kāsa	*Cayavanaprāśa*	*Ca.Ci. 1/62-74*
	Kāsa	*Harītakī Leha*	*Ca.Ci. 18/169*
	Kāsa	*Harītakī*	*Ca.Ci. 1/29-34*
21.	*Atisāra*	*Harītakī*	*Ca.Ci. 1/29-34*
	Atisāra	*Harītakī Prayoga*	*Ca.Ci. 19/17-18*
22.	*Chardi (Vamana)*	*Harītakī*	*Ca.Ci. 1/29-34*
23.	*Visarpa*	*Mustādi Yāpanā Vasti*	*Ca.Si. 12/15(1)*
24.	*Tṛṣṇā*	*Cayavanaprāśa*	*Ca.Ci. 1/1/62-74*
25.	*Viṣa*	*Yogarāja*	*Ca.Ci. 16/81-89*
26.	*Madātya*	*Balādi Yāpanā Vasti*	*Ca.Si. 12/15(5)*
27.	*Udāvarta*	*Madhwadi Vasti*	*Ca.Si. 12/13*
	Udāvarta	*Mustādi Yāpnā Vasti*	*Ca.Si. 12/15(1)*
	Udāvarta	*Harītakī*	*Ca.Ci. 1/29-34*
28.	*Ānāha*	*Harītakī*	*Ca.Ci. 1/29-34*
29.	*Mūtra Kṛchra*	*Madhu Ghṛtādī Vasti*	*Ca.Si. 12/14*
	Mūtra Kṛchra	*Goghṛtādi Vasti*	*Ca.Si. 12/12*
	Mūtra Kṛchra	*Mustādi Yāpnā Vasti*	*Ca.Si. 12/1*
30.	*Hṛdroga*	*Agastya Hrītakī*	*Ca.Ci. 18/57-62*
31.	*Śiroroga*	*Mustādi Yāpnā Vasti*	*Ca.Si. 12/15(1)*
32.	*Arucī*	*Yogarāja*	*Ca.Ci. 16/81-89*
	Arucī	*Agastya Harītakī*	*Ca.Ci. 18/57-62*
	Arucī	*Harītakī*	*Ca.Ci. 1/29-34*
33.	*Netra Roga*	*Droṅī Prāveṣika-Rasāyana*	*Ca.Ci. 1/4/7*
34.	*Nāsā Roga*	*Agastya Harītakī*	*Ca.Ci. 18/57-62*
	Nāsā Roga	*Pippalī Rasāyana*	*Ca.Ci. 1/3/32-35*

35.	*Karṇa Roga*	*Droṅī Prāveṣika-Rasāyana*	*Ca.Ci. 1/4/7*
36.	*Mukha Roga*	*Harītakī*	*Ca.Ci. 1/29-34*
37.	*Khālitya*	*Yamaka Anuvāsana Vasti*	*Ca.Si. 12/18(3)*
	Khālitya	*Catuha Sneha Anuvāsana Vasti*	*Ca.Si. 12/18(1)*
	Khālitya	*Agastya Harītakī*	*Ca.Ci. 12/57-62*
38.	*Vāta Vyādhi*	*Śatapāka-Sahastra Pāka Balā Taila*	*Ca.Ci. 29/119-120*
39.	*Ardita*	*Balādi Yāpnā Vasti*	*Ca.Si. 12/15(5)*
40.	*Āvṛta Vāta*	*Śilājatu*	*Ca.Ci. 28/241*
	Āvṛta Vāta	*Guggulu*	*Ca.Ci. 28/241*
41.	*Vāta Śoṅita*	*Mustādi Yāpnā Vasti*	*Ca.Si. 12/15(1)*
	Vāta Śoṅita	*Śata Pāka Sahastra Pāka Balā Taila*	*Ca.Ci. 29/119-120*
	Vāta Śoṅita	*Cayavanaprāśa*	*Ca.Ci. 1/1/62-74*
	Vāta Śoṅita	*Śilājatu*	*Ca.Ci. 29/15*
	Vāta Śoṅita	*Śudha Guggulu*	*Ca.Ci. 29/15*
42.	*Yoni Vayāpata*	*Catuha Sneha Anuvāsana Vasti*	*Ca.Si. 12/18(1)*
	Yoni Vayāpata	*Mustādi Yāpnā Vasti*	*Ca.Si. 12/15(1)*
	Yoni Vayāpata	*Śatapāka Sahastra Pāka Balā Taila*	*Ca.Ci. 29/119-120*
	Yoni Vayāpata	*Cayavanaprāśa*	*Ca.Çi. 1/1/62-74*
	Yoni Vayāpata	*Śīlajatu*	*Ca.Ci. 30/148*
43.	*Śukra Doṣa*	*Abhyāmalakī Rasāyana*	*Ca.Ci. 30/148*
	Śukra Doṣa	*Pippalī Rasāyana*	*Ca.Ci. 1/3/32-35*
	Śukra Doṣa	*Lauhādi Rasāyana*	*Ca.Ci. 1/3/15-23*
	Śukra Doṣa	*Triphalā Rasāyana*	*Ca.Ci. 1/3/42-47*
	Śukra Doṣa	*Bhallātaka Rasāyana*	*Ca.Ci. 1/2/13-22*

44.	*Napunsaktā*	*Yāpnā Rasāyana Vasti*	*Ca.Si. 12/1*
	Napunsaktā	*Rasāyana Kṣira-Sarpi*	*Ca.Ci. 30/203*
	Napunsaktā	*Rasāyana Vṛṣya Yoga*	*Ca.Ci. 30/203*
	Napunsaktā	*Harītakī*	*Ca.Ci. 1/29-34*

Note : *Ca* = *Caraka*
Ci = *Cikitsā*
Si = *Siddhi*

Chapter No. VII

Rasāyana described in *Suśruta Samhitā*

In addition to *Rasāyana* described by *Ācārya Caraka*, *Ācārya Suśruta* has described 18 types of "*Mahoṣdhis*" which are termed as "*Divya* (*Soma*) *Rasāyana*" which include following drugs.[1] These drugs are rare and their existence today is doubtful.

1. *Ajagarī*
2. *Śveta Kāpotī*
3. *Kṛṣṅa Kāpotī*
4. *Gonasī*
5. *Vārahī*
6. *Kanyā*
7. *Chatrā*
8. *Ati Chatrā*
9. *Kareṅu*

---

१. अथौषधीर्व्याख्यास्याम:–तत्राजगरी, श्वेतकापोती, कृष्णकापोती, गोनसी, वाराही, कन्या, छत्रा, अतिच्छत्रा, करेणु, अजा, चक्रका, आदित्यपर्णी, ब्रह्मसुर्वचला, श्रावणी, महाश्रावणी, गोलोमी, अजलोमी, महावेगवती, चेत्याष्टादश सोमसमवीर्या महौषधयो व्याख्याता:। तासौ सोमवत् क्रियाशी:स्तुतय: शास्त्रेऽभिहिता:। (सुश्रुत चिकित्सा-३०/४)

10. *Ajā*
11. *Cakrakā*
12. *Āditya Parṅī*
13. *Brahma Suvarcalā*
14. *Śrāvaṅī*
15. *Mahāśrāvaṅī*
16. *Golomī*
17. *Ajalomī*
18. *Mahāvegavatī*

Single *Rasāyana* Drugs Described in *Suśruta Samhitā*

S.N.	*Rasāyana Dravya*	Reference
1.	*Harītakī*	*Su.Sū. 44/62-63*
2.	*Jala*	*Su.Sū. 45/25-26*
3.	*Dugdha*	*Su.Sū. 45/49-52*
4.	*Ghṛta*	*Su.Sū 45/96*
5.	*Kālamegha*	*Su.Sū 45/125*
6.	*Gambhārī*	*Su.Sū. 46/184*
7.	*Mahati (Śatāvari)*	*Su.Sū. 46/300-302*
8.	*Varāhī Kanda*	*Su.Sū. 46/309*
9.	*Suvarṅa*	*Su.Sū. 46/326*
10.	*Śilājatu*	*Su.Ci. 13/4-16*
11.	*Anśumāṇa*	*Su.Ci. 29/5-8*
12.	*Munjawāna*	*Su.Ci. 29/5-8*
13.	*Candramā*	*Su.Ci. 29/5-8*
14.	*Rajata Prabha*	*Su.Ci. 29/5-8*
15.	*Dūrvā-Soma*	*Su.Ci. 29/5-8*
16.	*Kani Yāna*	*Su.Ci. 29/5-8*
17.	*Śvetakṣa*	*Su.Ci. 29/5-8*
18.	*Kanaka Prabhā*	*Su.Ci. 29/5-8*
19.	*Pratāna Vāta*	*Su.Ci. 29/5-8*
20.	*Tālavṛnta*	*Su.Ci. 29/5-8*
21.	*Karvīra*	*Su.Ci. 29/5-8*
22.	*Anśavāna*	*Su.Ci. 29/5-8*
23.	*Svayamaprabha*	*Su.Ci. 29/5-8*
24.	*Mahāsoma*	*Su.Ci. 29/5-8*
25.	*Garudāhṛta*	*Su.Ci. 29/5-8*
26.	*Traistubha*	*Su.Ci. 29/5-8*
27.	*Gāyatra*	*Su.Ci. 29/5-8*

28.	*Pākta*	*Su.Ci. 29/5-8*
29.	*Jāgata*	*Su.Ci. 29/5-8*
30.	*Śākawara*	*Su.Ci. 29/5-8*
31.	*Agniṣtoma*	*Su.Ci. 29/5-8*
32.	*Raiwata*	*Su.Ci. 29/5-8*
33.	*Tripadā Gāyatrī*	*Su.Ci. 29/5-8*
34.	*Udupati*	*Su.Ci. 29/5-8*
35.	*Ajagarī*	*Su.Ci. 30/5*
36.	*Śveta Kāpoti*	*Su.Ci. 30/5*
37.	*Kṛṣna Kāpoti*	*Su.Ci. 30/5*
38.	*Gonasī*	*Su.Ci. 30/5*
39.	*Vārāhī*	*Su.Ci. 30/5*
40.	*Kanyā*	*Su.Ci. 30/5*
41.	*Chatrā*	*Su.Ci. 30/5*
42.	*Atichatrā*	*Su.Ci. 30/5*
43.	*Kareṅu*	*Su.Ci. 30/5*
44.	*Ajā*	*Su.Ci. 30/5*
45.	Cakrakā	Su.Ci. 30/5
46.	Ādiyaparṅī	Su.Ci. 30/5
47.	*Brahma Suvarcalā*	*Su.Ci. 30/5*
48.	*Śrāvaṅī*	*Su.Ci. 30/5*
49.	*Mahāśrāvaṅī*	*Su.Ci. 30/5*
50.	*Golomī*	*Su.Ci. 30/5*
51.	*Ajalomī*	*Su.Ci. 30/5*
52.	*Mahāvegavatī*	*Su.Ci. 30/5*

Note: *Su* = *Suśruta*
Sū = *Sūtra*
Ci = *Cikitsā*

Rasāyana Yoga Described in Suśruta Samhitā

S.N.	*Rasāyana Yoga*	Reference
1.	*Śitala Jala, Dugdha, Madhu, Ghṛta Yoga*	*Su.Ci. 27/6*
2.	*Rasāyana Vidanga Tandula Yoga*	*Su.Ci. 27/7*
3.	*Vidanga Tandula Yoga (second)*	*Su.Ci. 27/8*
4.	*Gambhārī Yoga*	*Su.Ci. 27/9*
5.	*Balāmūla Rasāyana Yoga*	*Su.Ci. 27/10*
6.	*Vārāha Kanda Yoga*	*Su.Ci. 27/11*
7.	*Vijaya Sārādi Rasāyana Yoga*	*Su.Ci. 27/12*
8.	*Saṅphala Rasāyana Yoga*	*Su.Ci. 27/13*
9.	*Śveta Vākucī Rasāyana Yoga*	*Su.Ci. 28/3*
10.	*Kṛṣṅavākucī Rasāyana Yoga*	*Su.Ci. 28/3*
11.	*Citraka Haridrā Yoga*	*Su.Ci. 28/3*
12.	*Mandūkaparṅī Rasāyana Yoga*	*Su.Ci. 28/4*
13.	*Brāhmi Swarasa Rasāyana Yoga*	*Su.Ci. 28/5*
14.	*Brahmi Ghṛta Rasāyana Yoga*	*Su.Ci. 28/6*
15.	*Vacā Rasāyana Yoga*	*Su.Ci. 28/7*
16.	*Rasāyana Śatapāka Vacā Ghṛta*	*Su.Ci. 28/8*
17.	*Āyu Vardhaka Rasāyana*	*Su.Ci. 28/12*
18.	*Bīsa Kwātha Rasāyana Yoga*	*Su.Ci. 28/13*
19.	*Dāridrya Nāśaka Rasāyana Yoga*	*Su.Ci. 28/14*
20.	*Nilotpala Kwātha Rasāyana Yoga*	*Su.Ci. 28/15*
21.	*Rasāyana Smartha Prada Yoga*	*Su.Ci. 28/16*
22.	*Medhāvardhaka Vacādi Yoga*	*Su.Ci. 28/17*

23.	*Vāsā Taila Rasāyana Yoga*	*Su.Ci.* 28/18
24.	*Yavādi Yoga*	*Su.Ci.* 28/19
25.	*Ariṣta Śāmaka Madhwāda Yoga*	*Su.Ci.* 28/20
26.	*Vaśikaraṇa Śatāvarī Ghṛta*	*Su.Ci.* 28/21
27.	*Sobhāgya Kāraka Gocandanādi Yoga*	*Su.Ci.* 28/22
28.	*Sobhāgya Kāraka Padmādi Yoga*	*Su.Ci.* 28/23-24

Note : *Su* = *Suśruta* .
Ci = *Cikitsā*

Rasāyana* Therapy Indicated in Various Disorders in *Suśruta Samhitā

S.N.	Disorders	*Rasāyana* Used	Reference
1.	*Vraṅa*	*Harītakī*	*Su.Sū. 44/62-63*
2.	*Vāta Vyādhi*	*Godugdha*	*Su.Sū. 45/50-52*
	Vāta Vyādhi	*Ghṛta*	*Su.Sū. 45/96*
3.	*Arśa*	*Śilājatu*	*Su.Sū.13/15*
	Arśa	*Vidanga Tandula Yoga*	*Su.Ci. 27/7*
	Arśa	*Dugdha*	*Su.Sū. 5/55*
	Arśa	*Bhallātaka Vidhāna*	*Su.Ci. 6/17*
4.	*Aśmarī*	*Śilājatu*	*Su.Ci. 13/16*
5.	*Kuṣṭha*	*Śilājatu*	*Su.Ci. 13/14*
	Kuṣṭha	*Brāhmi Ghṛta*	*Su.Ci. 27/7*
	Kuṣṭha	*Vārāha Kanda*	*Su.Sū. 46/309*
6.	*Prameha*	*Śilājatu*	*Su.Ci. 13/14*
	Prameha	*Vāraha Kanda*	*Su.Sū. 46/309*
7.	*Udara Roga*	*Dugdha*	*Su.Sū. 45/53*
8.	*Apaci*	*Rasāyana Śatapāka Vacā Ghṛta*	*Su.Ci. 28/8*
9.	*Galaganda*	*Rasāyana Śatapāka Vacā Ghṛta*	*Su.Ci. 28/8*
10.	*Śotha*	*Śilājatu*	*Su.Ci. 13/15*
	Śotha	*Dugdha*	*Su.Sū. 45/53*
11.	*Netra Roga*	*Suvarṅa*	*Su.Sū. 46/325*
	Netra Roga	*Bījaka Sārādi Yoga*	*Su.Ci. 27/12*
	Netra Roga	*Vidanga Tandula Yoga* (second)	*Su.Ci. 27/8*

12.	*Graha (Bhūta Bādhā)*	*Vacā Rasāyana Yoga*	*Su.Ci. 28/6*
	Graha (BhūtaBādhā)	*Brāhmi Ghṛta Rasāyana Yoga*	*Su.Ci. 28/6*
13.	*Jwara*	*Dugdha*	*Su.Sū. 45/49*
	Jwara	*Ghṛta*	*Su.Sū. 45/96*
	Jwara	*Śilajatu*	*Su.Ci. 13/15*
14.	*Atisāra*	*Dugdha*	*Su.Sū. 45/49*
15.	*Pravāhikā*	*Dugdha*	*Su.Sū. 45/49*
16.	*Grahaṇī*	*Dugdha*	*Su.Sū. 45/49*
17.	*(a) Śoṣa*	*Śilājatu*	*Su.Ci. 13/15*
	Śoṣa	*Dugdha*	*Su.Sū. 45/49*
	Śoṣa	*Balāmūla Rasāyana Yoga*	*Su.Ci. 27/10*
	(b) Kṣaya	*Dugdha*	*Su.Sū. 45/49*
	(c) Kṣata	*Dugdha*	*Su.Sū. 45/49*
	(d) Kṣīṅa	*Dugdha*	*Su.Sū. 45/49*
18.	*Gulma*	*Dugdha*	*Su.Sū. 45/49*
	Gulma	*Śilājatu*	*Su.Ci. 13/15*
19.	*Śūla*	*Dugdha*	*Su.Sū. 45/49*
20.	*Hṛdroga*	*Dugdha*	*Su.Sū. 45/49*
	Hṛdroga	*Gambhāri Phala*	*Su.Sū. 46/184*
	Hṛdroga	*Suvarṅa*	*Su.Sū. 46/326*
21.	*Pāndū*	*Dugdha*	*Su.Sū. 45/49*
	Pāndū	*Śilājatu*	*Su.Ci. 13/15*

22.	*Rakta Pitta*	*Dugdha*	*Su.Sū.* 45/49
	Rakta Pitta	*Gambhārī*	*Su.Sū.* 46/184
	Rakta Pitta	*Balāmūla Rasāyana*	*Su.Sū.* 27/10
23.	*Mūrchā*	*Dugdha*	*Su.Sū.* 45/49
24.	*Mada*	*Dugdha*	*Su.Sū.* 45/49
25.	*Dāha*	*Dugdha*	*Su.Sū.* 45/49
26.	*Tṛṣṅā*	*Dugdha*	*Su.Sū.* 45/49
27.	*Śwāsa*	*Dugdha*	*Su.Sū.* 45/49
28.	*Kāsa*	*Dugdha*	*Su.Sū.* 45/49
29.	*Kṛmi*	*Vidanga TandulaYoga*	*Su.Ci.* 27/7
	Kṛmi	*Vidanga Tandula Yoga* (second)	*Su.Ci.* 27/8
	Kṛmi	*Vārāha Kanda*	*Su.Sū.* 46/309
30.	*Udāvarta*	*Dugdha*	*Su.Sū.* 45/49
	Udāvarta	*Ghṛta*	*Su.Sū.* 45/96
31.	*Ānāha*	*Ghṛta*	*Su.Sū.* 45/96
32.	*Mūtra Vivandha*	*Gambhārī*	*Su.Sū.* 46/184
33.	*Apasmāra*	*Ghṛta*	*Su.Sū.* 45/96
	Apasmāra	*Śilājatu*	*Su.Ci.* 13/14
	Apasmāra	*Brāhmi Ghṛta Rasāyana*	*Su.Ci.* 28/6
34.	*Unmāda*	*Dugdha*	*Su.Sū.* 45/49
	Unmāda	*Ghṛta*	*Su.Sū.* 45/96
	Unmāda	*Śilājatu*	*Su.Ci.* 13/14

35.	*Viṣa*	*Brāhmī Ghṛta Rasāyana Yoga*	*Su.Ci.* 28/6
	Viṣa	*Ghṛta*	*Su.Sū.* 45/96
	Viṣa	*Śilājatu*	*Su.Ci.* 13/14
36.	*Yoni Roga*	*Dugdha*	*Su.Sū.* 45/49
37.	*Ślipada*	*Śilājatu*	*Su.Ci.* 13/14
	Ślipada	*Rasāyana Śatapāka Vacā Yoga*	*Su.Ci.* 28/8

Note : *Su* = *Suśruta*
Ci = *Cikitsā*
Sū = *Sūtra*

Chapter VIII

Rasāyana Described in *Aṣṭānga Sangraha*

Single *Rasāyana* Drugs Described in *Aṣṭānga Sangraha*

S.N.	*Rasāyana Dravya*	Reference
1.	*Dugdha*	*A.S.Sū. 6/54*
2.	*Kākamāci*	*A.S.Sū. 7/115*
3.	*Vidāri Kanda*	*A.S.Sū. 7/130*
4.	*Laśuna*	*A.S.Sū. 7/162-164*
5.	*Gambhāri*	*A.S.Sū. 7/178*
6.	*Suvarṅa*	*A.S.Sū. 12/12*
7.	*Śilājatu*	*A.S.Sū. 12/27*
8.	*Pippalī*	*A.S.Sū. 12/51-52*
9.	*Amṛtā*	*A.S.Sū. 12/71*
10.	*Guggulu*	*A.S.Sū. 12/74*
11.	*Nāgabalā Rasāyana*	*A.S.Sū. 5/71-75*
12.	*Harītakī*	*A.S.U. 49/17-20*
13.	*Mandūkaparṅī*	*A.S.U. 49/42*
14.	*Madhuyaṣṭi*	*A.S.U. 49/42*
15.	*Guducī*	*A.S.U. 49/42*

16.	*Śankhapuṣpī*	*A.S.U. 49/42*
17.	*Atibalā*	*A.S.U. 49/48*
18.	*Candana*	*A.S.U. 49/48*
19.	*Agaru*	*A.S.U. 49/48*
20.	*Dhava*	*A.S.U. 49/48*
21.	*Tiniśa*	*A.S.U. 49/48*
22.	*Khadira*	*A.S.U. 49/48*
23.	*Viṭṭa Khadira*	*A.S.U. 49/48*
24.	*Śāka*	*A.S.U. 49/48*
25.	*Śinśapa*	*A.S.U. 49/48*
26.	*Asana*	*A.S.U. 49/48*
27.	*Tulasī*	*A.S.U. 49/48*
28.	*Punarnavā*	*A.S.U. 49/48*
29.	*Anantā*	*A.S.U. 49/48*
30.	*Vidārī*	*A.S.U. 49/48*
31.	*Gokṣura*	*A.S.U. 49/48*
32.	*Aśwagandhā*	*A.S.U. 49/48*
33.	*Varāha Kanda*	*A.S.U. 49/48*
34.	*Śatāvarī*	*A.S.U. 49/48*
35.	*Āmalakī*	*A.S.U. 49/14*
37.	*Ghṛta*	*A.S.Sū. 6/75*

Note : *A.* = *Aṣṭānga*

S. = *Sangraha*

Sū. = *Sūtra*

U. = *Uttara Tantra*

Rasāyana Yoga Described In _Aṣṭānga Sangraha_

S.N.	*Rasāyana Yoga*	Reference
1.	*Triphalā Rasāyana*	*A.S.Sū. 12/47*
2.	*Kuṣmānda Rasāyana*	*A.S.Ci. 5/68*
3.	*Nāgabalā Ghṛta*	*A.S.Ci. 5/71-75*
4.	*Agastya Leha*	*A.S.Ci. 5/82-87*
5.	*Vaṣiṣṭa Muni Prokta Rasāyana*	*A.S.Ci. 7/48-52*
6.	*Sarpi Guḍa*	*A.S.Ci. 7/48-52*
7.	*Yogarāja Rasāyana*	*A.S.Ci. 21/14*
8.	*Madhu Tailika Rasāyana Vasti*	*A.S.K. 5/3*
9.	*Mustādi Yāpnā Vasti*	*A.S.K. 5/11*
10.	*Sahacarādi Rasāyana*	*A.S.K. 5/24*
11.	*Śirīṣa Taila*	*A.S.U. 10/17*
12.	*Brahma Rasāyana*	*A.S.U. 49/21*
13.	*Abhyāmalakādi Ghṛta*	*A.S.U. 49/22*
14.	*Droṅī Prāveśika Āmalakī*	*A.S.U. 49/24*
15.	*Abhyāmalaka Pippalayādī Rasāyana*	*A.S.U. 49/25*
16.	*Āmalakī Rasāyana*	*A.S.U. 49/23*
17.	*Vidanga Tandulādi Rasāyana*	*A.S.U. 49/27*
18.	*Abhyāmalaka Vibhitaka Vividha Yoga*	*A.S.U. 49/28*
19.	*Cayavanaprāśa*	*A.S.U. 49/29*
20.	*Triphalādi Rasāyana*	*A.S.U. 49/30*
21.	*Triphalā Lepa Rasāyana Yoga*	*A.S.U. 49/31*
22.	*Harītakī, Vibhitaka,Āmalaka Yoga*	*A.S.U. 49/32*
23.	*Āysāmalakī Rasāyana*	*A.S.U. 49/33*

24.	*Tāmra Rajat Suvarṅa Yoga (Āmalakī Rasa Bhāvita)*	*A.S.U. 49/34*
25.	*Suvarṅa-Āmalakī Madhu Yoga*	*A.S.U. 49/35*
26.	*Suvarṅa Padama Bījādi Rasāyana* (First and second)	*A.S.U. 49/36-37*
27.	*Madhu Pippalyādi Yoga*	*A.S.U. 49/38*
28.	*Suvarṅa Bilwādi Yoga*	*A.S.U. 49/39*
29.	*Suvarṅa Mākṣika Śatāvari Ghṛta Yoga*	*A.S.U. 49/40*
30.	*Suvarṅa Śankhapuṣpi Yoga*	*A.S.U. 49/41*
31.	*Suvarṅa Vacā Yoga*	*A.S.U. 49/41*
32.	*Suvarṅa Kamala Keśara Yoga*	*A.S.U. 49/41*
33.	*Suvarṅa Vidāri Yoga*	*A.S.U. 49/41*
34.	*Nalada Śankhapuṣpayādi Yoga*	*A.S.U. 49/43*
35.	*Pancārvinda Ghṛta*	*A.S.U. 49/45*
36.	*Catuṣkuvalaya Ghṛta*	*A.S.U. 49/45*
37.	*Brāhmī Vacādi Yoga*	*A.S.U. 49/46*
38.	*Nāgabalā Yoga*	*A.S.U. 49/47*
39.	*Tuvaraka Taila* (first & second)	*A.S.U. 49/53*
40.	*Tuvarakānjana*	*A.S.U. 49/55*
41.	*Tuvaraka Yoga*	*A.S.U. 49/54*
42.	*Bhallātaka Yoga (vividha)*	*A.S.U. 49/58*
43.	*Vardhamāna Bhallātaka Yoga*	*A.S.U. 49/59*
44.	*Sahastra Dravya Bhallātaka Yoga*	*A.S.U. 49/60*
45.	*Bhallātaka Yoga* (Three)	*A.S.U. 49/61-63*
46.	*Bhallātaka Tailādi Yoga*	*A.S.U. 49/64*

47.	*Bhallātaka Sarpi*	*A.S.U. 49/65*
48.	*Bhallātaka Taila*	*A.S.U. 49/66*
49.	*Bhallātaka (Vividha Yoga)*	*A.S.U. 49/67*
50.	*Pippalī Vardhamāna* (two)	*A.S.U. 49/71-72*
51.	*Vidanga Vividha Yoga*	*A.S.U. 49/74*
52.	*Alambuśā Prayoga*	*A.S.U. 49/75*
53.	*Somarājī Yoga*	*A.S.U. 49/76*
54.	*Vākucī Yoga* (second, third & fourth)	*A.S.U. 49/77*
55.	*Vākucī Vividha Yoga*	*A.S.U. 49/77-96*
56.	*Vacā Kalpa (Kṛṣaṅa, Śveta)*	*A.S.U. 49/97-98*
57.	*Vacā Ghṛta*	*A.S.U. 49/99*
58.	*Laśuna Yoga*	*A.S.U. 49/100*
59.	*Laśuna Vividha Yoga*	*A.S.U. 49/101-135*
60.	*Kukkutī Yoga Vividha*	*A.S.U.49/142-150*
61.	*Kancukī Vividha Yoga*	*A.S.U.49/151-157*
62.	*Somāmṛta Ghṛta*	*A.S.U.49/158*
63.	*Vividha Guggulu Yoga*	*A.S.U.49/159-178*
64.	*Śilājatu Yoga (Vividha)*	*A.S.U.49/179-197*
65.	*Suvarṅa Mākṣika Yoga*	*A.S.U.49/198-206*
66.	*Vṛdha Daraka*	*A.S.U.49/207-217*
67.	*Kuṣṭha Prayoga*	*A.S.U. 49/218*
68.	*Haritkyādi Yoga* (second)	*A.S.U. 49/222-23*
69.	*Triphalādi Yoga* (first & second)	*A.S.U. 49/224-25*
70.	*Harītakī Vidangādi Yoga*	*A.S.U. 49/226*
71.	*Bījakādi Yoga*	*A.S.U. 49/227*
72.	*Triphalā Kaṣāyādi Yoga*	*A.S.U. 49/228-29*

73.	*Āmalakī Yoga*	*A.S.U. 49/231*
74.	*Dhātrayādi Yoga (Vividha)*	*A.S.U. 49/232*
75.	*Śwadanṣtrāmalaki Yoga*	*A.S.U. 49/234*
76.	*Vidanga Madhuyaṣṭyādi Yoga*	*A.S.U. 49/235*
77.	*Vidanga Bhallātakādi Yoga*	*A.S.U. 49/236*
78.	*Vidanga Vividha Yoga*	*A.S.U.49/237-239*
79.	*Punarnavā Yoga*	*A.S.U. 49/240*
80.	*Mūrvādi Vividha Yoga*	*A.S.U. 49/241*
81.	*Śatāvari Ghṛta*	*A.S.U. 49/242*
82.	*Aśwagandhā Yoga*	*A.S.U. 49/243*
83.	*Śilajatwādi Yoga*	*A.S.U. 49/245*
84.	*Madhwādi Yoga*	*A.S.U. 49/246*
85.	*Narsingha Ghṛta*	*A.S.U. 49/247-48*
86.	*Gambhārī Yoga*	*A.S.U. 49/250*

Note : *A* = *Aṣṭānga*
Sū = *Sūtra*
Ci = *Cikitsā*
K = *Kalpa Sthāna*
U = *Uttara Tantra*

Rasāyana Therapy Indicated in Various Disorders in *Aṣṭānga Sangraha*

S.N.	*Disorders*	*Rasāyana Used*	*Reference*
1.	*Jwara*	*Dugdha*	*A.S.Sū. 6/54*
	Jwara	*Amṛta*	*A.S.Sū. 12/71*
	Jwara	*Kuṣmānda Rasāyana*	*A.S.Ci. 5/68*
	Jwara	*Agastya Leha*	*A.S.Ci. 5/82-87*
	Jwara	*Pippalī Vardhamāna Rasāyana*	*A.S.U. 49/73*
	Jwara	*Yoga Rāj Rasāyana*	*A.S.Ci. 21/14*
	Jwara	*Mustādi Yāpanā Vasti*	*A.S.K. 5/11*
	Jwara	*Sahacarādi Rasāyana Yoga*	*A.S.K. 5/24*
	Jwara	*Śirīṣa Taila*	*A.S.U. 10/17*
	Jwara	*Cayavanaprāśa*	*A.S.U. 49/29*
	Jwara	*Brāhmi Vacādī Yoga*	*A.S.U. 49/46*
	Jwara	*Pippalī Vardhamāna Rasāyana*	*A.S.U. 49/70-73*
	Jwara	*Somāmṛta Ghṛta*	*A.S.U. 49/158*
	Jwara	*Śilājatu Vividha Yoga*	*A.S.U. 49/189*
	Jwara	*Śivā Gutikā*	*A.S.U. 49/193*
	Jwara	*Swarṅa Mākṣika (Vividha Yoga)*	*A.S.U. 49/199*
2.	*Rakta Pitta*	*Dugdha*	*A.S.Sū. 6/56*
	RaktaPitta	*Kuṣmānda Rasāyana*	*A.S.Ci. 5/67*
	RaktaPitta	*Nāgabalā Ghṛta*	*A.S.Ci. 5/74*
	RaktaPitta	*Śilājatū Vividha Yoga*	*A.S.U. 49/189*
3.	*Kāsa*	*Dugdha*	*A.S.Sū. 6/56*

	Kāsa	*Lahasuna*	*A.S.Sū. 7/165*
	Kāsa	*Pippalī*	*A.S.Sū. 12/52*
	Kāsa	*Pippalī Vardhamāna Rasāyana*	*A.S.U. 49/73*
	Kāsa	*Kuṣmānda Rasāyana*	*A.S.Ci. 5/67*
	Kāsa	*Agastya Leha*	*A.S.Ci. 5/87*
	Kāsa	*Mustādi Yāpna Vasti*	*A.S.K. 5/11*
	Kāsa	*Cayavanaprāśa*	*A.S.U. 49/29*
	Kāsa	*Alāmbuśa Prayoga*	*A.S.U. 49/75*
	Kāsa	*Vākucī Vividha Yoga*	*A.S.U. 49/78*
	Kāsa	*Lahaśuna Vividha Yoga*	*A.S.U. 49/123*
	Kāsa	*Śivā Gutikā*	*A.S.U. 49/193*
	Kāsa	*Śilājatu*	*A.S.Sū. 12/27*
4.	*Kṣata Kṣaya*	*Śilājatu*	*A.S.Sū. 12/27*
	Kṣata Kṣaya	*Kuṣmānda Rasāyana*	*A.S.Ci. 5/67*
	Kṣata Kṣaya	*Nāgabalā Ghṛta*	*A.S.Ci. 5/74*
	Kṣata Kṣaya	*Agastya Leha*	*A.S.Sū. 5/87*
	Kṣata Kṣaya	*Sarpī Guḍa*	*A.S.Ci. 7/53*
	Kṣata Kṣaya	*Cayavanaprāśa*	*A.S.U. 49/29*
5.	*Śwāsa*	*Dugdha*	*A.S.Sū. 6/55*
	Śwāsa	*Kuṣmānda Rasāyana*	*A.S.Ci. 5/67*
	Śwāsa	*Agastya Leha*	*A.S.Ci. 5/87*

	Śwāsa	*Yogarāja Rasāyana*	*A.S.Ci. 21/14*
	Śwāsa	*Lahaśuna*	*A.S.Sū. 7/165*
	Śwāsa	*Cayavanaprāśa*	*A.S.U. 49/29*
	Śwāsa	*Pippalī Vardhamāna Rasāyana*	*A.S.U. 49/73*
	Śwāsa	*Vākucī Vividha Yoga*	*A.S.U. 49/78*
	Śwāsa	*Lahaśuna Vividha Yoga*	*A.S.U.49/123*
	Śwāsa	*Guggulu-Vividha Yoga*	*A.S.U.49/165*
	Śwāsa	*Śivā Gutikā*	*A.S.U. 49/193*
6.	*Hikkā*	*Lahśuna*	*A.S.Sū. 7/165*
	Hikkā	*Śilājatu*	*A.S.Sū. 12/27*
	Hikkā	*Kuṣmānda Rasāyana*	*A.S.Ci. 5/67*
	Hikkā	*Agastya Leha*	*A.S.Ci. 5/87*
	Hikkā	*Pippalī Vardhamāna Rasāyana*	*A.S.U. 49/73*
	Hikkā	*Śivā Gutikā*	*A.S.U. 49/193*
7.	*Rājayakṣmā*	*Ajā Dugdhādi Rasāyana*	*A.S.Ci. 7/104*
	Rājayakṣmā	*Pippalī Vardhamāna Rasāyana*	*A.S.U. 49/73*
	Rājayakṣmā	*Śilājatu Vividha Yoga*	*A.S.U. 49/189*
	Rājayakṣmā	*Suvarṅa Mākṣika Vividha Yoga*	*A.S.U. 49/199*
	Rājayakṣmā	*Yogarāja Rasāyana*	*A.S.Ci. 21/14(Kha)*
8.	*Chardi*	*Pippalī Vardhamāna Rasāyana*	*A.S.U. 49/73*
	Chardi	*Śīvā Gutikā*	*A.S.U. 49/193*
9.	*Hṛdroga*	*Agastya Leha*	*A.S.Ci.5/87*

	Hṛdroga	*Cayavanaprāśa*	*A.S.U.*	*49/29*
	Hṛdroga	*Śivā Gutikā*	*A.S.U.*	*49/193*
10.	*Tṛṣṅā*	*Dugdha*	*A.S.Sū.*	*6/55*
	Tṛṣṅā	*Amṛtā*	*A.S.Sū.*	*12/71*
	Tṛṣṅā	*Nāgabalā Ghṛta*	*A.S.Ci.*	*5/75*
11.	*Mada Madātya*	*Śirīṣa Taila*	*A.S.U.*	*10/17*
	Mada Madātya	*Śivā Gutikā*	*A.S.U.*	*49/199-206*
	Mada Madātya	*Dugdha*	*A.S.Sū.*	*6/55*
12.	*Arśa*	*Lahaśuna*	*A.S.Sū.*	*7/165*
	Arśa	*Agastya Leha*	*A.S.Ci.*	*5/87*
	Arśa	*Śuṇṭhayādi Rasāyana*	*A.S.Sū.*	*10/13*
	Arśa	*Yogarāja Rasāyana*	*A.S.Ci.*	*21/14*
	Arśa	*Madhu Tailika Vasti*	*A.S.K.*	*5/3*
	Arśa	*Mustādi Yāpnā Vasti*	*A.S.K.*	*5/11*
	Arśa	*Bhallātaka Tailādiyoga*	*A.S.U.*	*49/64*
	Arśa	*Bhallātaka Vividha Yoga*	*A.S.U.*	*49/58*
	Arśa	*Pippalī Vardhamāna Rasāyana*	*A.S.U.*	*49/73*
	Arśa	*Vidanga Vividha Yoga*	*A.S.U.*	*49/74*
	Arśa	*Vākucī Vividha Yoga*	*A.S.U.*	*49/78*
	Arśa	*Lahaśuna Vividha Yoga*	*A.S.U.*	*49/123*
	Arśa	*Śivā Gutikā*	*A.S.U.*	*49/193*
	Arśa	*Vṛdha Drakṣā Vividha Yoga*	*A.S.U.*	*49/213*

	Arśa	*Śilājatu*	*A.S.Sū. 12/28*
13.	*Atisāra*	*Śivā Gutikā*	*A.S.U. 49/193*
14.	*Grahaṅī*	*Agastya Leha*	*A.S.Ci. 5/87*
	Grahaṅī	*Yogarāja Rasāyana*	*A.S.Ci. 21/24*
	Grahaṅī	*Pippali Vardhamāna Rasāyana*	*A.S.U. 49/73*
	Grahaṅī	*Śivā Gutikā*	*A.S.U. 49/193*
15.	*Mūtra Roga*	*Śivā Gutika*	*A.S.U. 49/193*
	Mūtrā Ghāta	*Śivā Gutika*	*A.S.U. 49/193*
	Mutra Kṛchra	*Śilājatu*	*A.S.Sū. 12/28*
	Mutra Kṛchra	*Dugdha*	*A.S.Su. 6/55*
	Mutra Kṛchra	*Cayavanaprāśa*	*A.S.U. 49/29*
16.	*Prameha*	*Lahaśuna*	*A.S.Sū. 7/165*
	Prameha	*Śilājatu*	*A.S.Sū. 12/28*
	Prameha	*Triphalā Rasāyana*	*A.S.Sū. 12/47*
	Prameha	*Guggulu*	*A.S.Sū. 12/75*
	Prameha	*Agastya leha*	*A.S.Ci. 5/87*
	Prameha	*Sarpi Guḍa*	*A.S.Ci. 7/52*
	Prameha	*Yogarāja Rasāyana*	*A.S.Ci. 21/14*
	Prameha	*Madhu Tailika Vasti*	*A.S.K. 5/3*
	Prameha	*Mustādi Yāpnā Vasti*	*A.S.K. 5/11*
	Prameha	*Śirīṣa Taila*	*A.S.U. 10/17*
	Prameha	*Bhallātaka Vividha Yoga*	*A.S.U. 49/58*

	Prameha	*Vidanga Vividha Yoga*	*A.S.U. 49/74*
	Prameha	*Vākuci Vividha Yoga*	*A.S.U. 49/78*
	Prameha	*Lahasuna Vividha Yoga*	*A.S.U. 49/123*
	Prameha	*Guggulu Vividha Yoga*	*A.S.U. 49/170*
	Prameha	*Plāndu*	*A.S.U. 49/138*
	Prameha	*Śilājatu Vividha Yoga*	*A.S.U. 49/192*
	Prameha	*Suvarṅa Makṣika Vividha Yoga*	*A.S.U. 49/199*
17.	*Vidradhi*	*Guggulu Vividha Yoga*	*A.S.U. 49/165*
	Vidradhi	*Śivā Gutikā*	*A.S.U. 49/193*
18.	*Vṛdhi (Vividha)*	*Madhu Tailika Vasti*	*A.S.K. 5/3*
	Vṛdhi (Vividha)	*Vākucī Vividha Yoga*	*A.S.U. 49/78*
	Vṛdhi (Vividha)	*Guggula Viviuha Yoga*	*A.S.U. 49/165*
	Vṛdhi (Vividha)	*Vṛdha Drakṣā Vividha Yoga*	*A.S.U. 49/214*
19.	*Gulma*	*Lahaśuna*	*A.S.Sū. 7/165*
	Gulma	*Agastya Leha*	*A.S.Ci. 5/87*
	Gulma	*Sarpi Guḍa*	*A.S.Ci. 7/52*
	Gulma	*Yogarāja Rasāyana*	*A.S.Ci. 21/14*
	Gulma	*Madhu Tailika Vasti*	*A.S.K. 5/3*
	Gulma	*Mustādi Yāpnā Vasti*	*A.S.K. 5/11*
	Gulma	*Śirīṣa Taila*	*A.S.U. 10/17*
	Gulma	*Brāhmī Vacādi Yoga*	*A.S.U. 49/46*
	Gulma	*Alāmbuśa Prayoga*	*A.S.U. 49/75*
	Gulma	*Vākucī Vividha Yoga*	*A.S.U. 49/77-98*

	Gulma	*Lahaśuna Vividha Yoga*	*A.S.U. 49/123*
	Gulma	*Guggula Vivivdha Yoga*	*A.S.U. 49/165*
	Gulma	*Śivā Gutikā*	*A.S.U. 49/193*
	Gulma	*Vṛdha Drakṣā Vividha Yoga*	*A.S.U. 49/213*
20.	*Udara Roga*	*Brāhmi Vacādi Yoga*	*A.S.U. 49/46*
	Udara Roga	*Guggula Vividha Yoga*	*A.S.U. 49/165*
	Udara Roga	*Śilājatu Vividha Yoga*	*A.S.U. 49/189*
	Udara Roga	*Śivā Gutika*	*A.S.U. 49/193*
	Udara Roga	*Vṛdha Drākṣā vividha Yoga*	*A.S.U. 49/214*
21.	*Pāndu Roga*	*Śilājatu*	*A.S.U. 49/189*
	Pāndu Roga	*Yogarāja Rasāyana*	*A.S.Ci. 21/14*
	Pāndu Roga	*Śirīṣa Taila*	*A.S.U. 10/17*
	Pāndu Roga	*Pippalī Vardhamāna Rasāyana*	*A.S.U. 49/73*
	Pāndu Roga	*Śilājatu Vividha Yoga*	*A.S.U. 49/189*
	Pāndu Roga	*Śivā Gutikā*	*A.S.U. 49/193*
	Pāndu Roga	*Vākucī Vividha Yoga*	*A.S.U. 49/78*

	Pāndu Roga	*Suvarṅa Mākṣika Vividha Yoga*	*A.S.U. 49/199*
	Pāndu Roga	*Sarpi Guḍa*	*A.S.Ci. 7/52*
	Pāndu Roga	*Guggula Vividha Yoga*	*A.S.U. 49/170*
22.	*Śavathū (Śopha)*	*Śilājatu*	*A.S.U. 49/189*
	Śavathū	*Guggula*	*A.S.U. 49/170*
	Śavathū	*Mustādi Yapnā Vasti*	*A.S.K. 5/11*
	Śavathū	*Cayavanaprāśa*	*A.S.U. 49/29*
	Śavathū	*Pippalī Vardhamāna Rasāyana*	*A.S.U. 49/73*
	Śavathū	*Vākucī Vividha yoga*	*A.S.U. 49/90*
	Śavathū	*Śilājatu Vividha Yoga*	*A.S.U. 49/189*
	Śavathū	*Suvarṅa Mākṣika Vividha Yoga*	*A.S.U. 49/199*
23.	*Visarpa*	*Mustādi Yāpnā Vasti*	*A.S.K. 5/11*
	Visarpa	*Śirīṣa Taila*	*A.S.U. 10/17*
24.	*Kuṣṭha*	*Kākamaci*	*A.S.Sū. 7/115*
	Kuṣṭha	*Lahasuna*	*A.S.Sū. 7/165*
	Kuṣṭha	*Yogarāja Rasāyana*	*A.S.Ci. 21/14*
	Kuṣṭha	*Tuvaraka*	*A.S.Ci. 21/8,24*
	Kuṣṭha	*Bhallātaka*	*A.S.Ci. 21/8,24*
	Kuṣṭha	*Alamavuśā*	*A.S.Ci. 21/24*
	Kuṣṭha	*Avālaguja*	*A.S.Ci. 21/24*
	Kuṣṭha	*Brāhmi Vacādi Yoga*	*A.S.U. 49/46*
	Kuṣṭha	*Tuvaraka Taila*	*A.S.U. 49/57*

	Kuṣṭha	*Bhallātaka Yoga (Vividha)*	*A.S.U. 49/58*
	Kuṣṭha	*Bhallātaka Tailādi Yoga*	*A.S.U. 49/64*
	Kuṣṭha	*Vidanga Vividha Yoga*	*A.S.U. 49/74*
	Kuṣṭha	*Vākucī Vividha Yoga*	*A.S.U. 49/78*
	Kuṣṭha	*Lahaśuna Vividha Yoga*	*A.S.U. 49/123*
	Kuṣṭha	*Vṛdha Drakṣā Vividha Yoga*	*A.S.U. 49/213*
25.	*Świtra*	*Vākucī Vividha Yoga*	*A.S.U. 49/85*
	Świtra	*Guggulu Vividha Yoga*	*A.S.U. 49/170*
	Świtra	*Śivā Gutikā*	*A.S.U. 49/193*
26.	*Kṛmi*	*Lahasuna*	*A.S.Sū. 7/165*
	Kṛmi	*Guggulu*	*A.S.Sū. 12/74*
	Kṛmi	*Yogarāja Rasāyana*	*A.S.Ci. 21/14*
	Kṛmi	*Madhu Tailika Vasti*	*A.S.K. 5/3*
	Kṛmi	*Bhallātaka Yoga (Vividha)*	*A.S.U. 49/58*
	Kṛmi	*Vākucī Vividha Yoga*	*A.S.U. 49/78*
	Kṛmi	*Lahaśuna Vividha Yoga*	*A.S.U. 49/123*
	Kṛmi	*Guggula Vividha Yoga*	*A.S.U. 49/171*
27.	*Vāta Vyādhi*	*Lahaśuna*	*A.S.Sū. 7/165*
	Vāta Vyādhi	*Pippalī*	*A.S.Sū. 12/52*
	Vāta Vyādhi	*Guggulu*	*A.S.Sū. 12/74*
	Vāta Vyādhi	*Cayavanaprāśa*	*A.S.U. 49/29*
	Vāta Vyādhi	*Brāhmī Vacādi Yoga*	*A.S.U. 49/46*

	Vāta Vyādhi	*Lahaśuna Vividha Yoga*	*A.S.U. 49/122*
	Vāta Vyādhi	*Kukkatī Vividha Yoga*	*A.S.U. 49/144*
	Vāta Vyādhi	*Guggulu Vividha Yoga*	*A.S.U. 49/169*
28.	*Vāta Śoṅita*	*Cayavanaprāśa*	*A.S.U. 49/29*
	Vāta Śoṅita	*Brāhma Rasāyana*	*A.S.Ci. 24/34*
	Vāta Śoṅita	*Mustādi Yāpnā Vasti*	*A.S.K. 5/11*
	Vāta Śoṅita	*Śirīṣa Taila*	*A.S.U. 10/17*
	Vāta Śoṅita	*Pippalī Vardhamāna Rasāyana*	*A.S.U. 49/73*
	Vāta Śoṅita	*Śivā Gutikā*	*A.S.U. 49/193*
	Vāta Śoṅita	*Gudvcyādi Vividha Rasāyana Yoga*	*A.S.Ci. 24/15*
29.	*Graha*	*Śirīṣa Taila*	*A.S.U. 10/17*
	Graha	*Vacā Ghṛta*	*A.S.U. 49/99*
	Graha	*Somamṛta Ghṛta*	*A.S.U. 49/158*
	Graha	*Vṛdha Drākṣā Vividha Yoga*	*A.S.U. 49/208*
30.	*Bhūta Bādhā*	*Vākucī Vividha Yoga*	*A.S.U. 49/95*
31.	*Unmāda*	*Mustādi Yāpnā Vasti*	*A.S.K. 5/11*
	Unmāda	*Śirīṣa Taila*	*A.S.U. 10/17*

Unmāda	*Brāhmī Vacādi Yoga*	*A.S.U. 49/56*
Unmāda	*Vacā Ghṛta*	*A.S.U. 49/99*
Unmāda	*Śilājatu Vividha Yoga*	*A.S.U. 49/189*
Unmāda	*Śivā Gutikā*	*A.S.U. 49/193*
Unmāda	*Vṛdha Drākṣā Vivdha Yoga*	*A.S.U. 49/208*
32. *Apasmāra*	*Śirīṣa Taila*	*A.S.U. 10/17*
Apasmāra	*Vacā Ghṛta*	*A.S.U. 49/99*
Apasmāra	*Śilājatu Vividha Yoga*	*A.S.U. 49/189*
Apasmāra	*Śivā Gutikā*	*A.S.U. 49/193*
Apasmāra	*Vṛdha Drākṣā Vividha Yoga*	*A.S.U. 49/208*
33. *Netra Roga*	*Triphalā Rasāyana*	*A.S.Sū. 12/47*
Netra Roga	*Mustādi Yāpnā Vasti*	*A.S.K. 5/11*
Netra Roga	*Tuvaraka Taila*	*A.S.U. 49/55*
Netra Roga	*Kancukī Vividha Yoga*	*A.S.U. 49/154-155*
Netra Roga	*Guggula Vividha Yoga*	*A.S.U. 49/178*
Netra Roga	*Śivā Gutikā*	*A.S.U. 49/193*
Netra Roga	*Suvarṇa Mākṣika Vividha Yoga*	*A.S.U. 49/199*
Netra Roga	*Kuṣṭha Vividha Yoga*	*A.S.U. 49/218*
Netra Roga	*Sarpi Guḍa*	*A.S.Ci. 7/52*

34.	*Karṅa Roga*	*Guggula Vividha Yoga*	*A.S.U. 49/165*
	Karṅa Roga	*Suvarṇamakṣika Vividha Yoga*	*A.S.U. 49/199*
	Karṅa Roga	*Kuṣṭha Vividha Yoga*	*A.S.U. 49/2/8*
35.	*Nāsā Roga*	*Pippalī Vardhamāna Rasāyana*	*A.S.Ci. 17/13*
	Nāsā Roga	*Lahaśuna*	*A.S.Sū. 7/165*
	Nāsā Roga	*Agastya Leha*	*A.S.Sū. 5/87*
	Nāsā Roga	*Vākucī Vividha Yoga*	*A.S.U. 49/78*
	Nāsā Roga	*Śivā Gutikā*	*A.S.U. 49/193*
36.	*Mukha Roga*	*Śivā Gutikā*	*A.S.U. 49/193*
37.	*Śiroroga*	*Guggula Vividha Yoga*	*A.S.U. 49/165*
	Śiroroga	*Śivā Gutikā*	*A.S.U. 49/193*
	Śiroroga	*Kancukī Vividha Yoga*	*A.S.U. 49/155*
38.	*Vraṅa*	*Guggula Vividha Yoga*	*A.S.U. 49/170*
39.	*Bhagandara*	*Sarpi Guḍa*	*A.S.Ci. 7/52*
	Bhagandara	*Alāmbuśa Prayoga*	*A.S.U. 49/75*
	Bhagandara	*Vākucī Vividha Yoga*	*A.S.U. 49/88*
	Bhagandara	*Guggula Vividha Yoga*	*A.S.U. 49/170*
	Bhagandara	*Śivā Gutikā*	*A.S.U. 49/193*

40.	*Granthi*	*Guggulu*	*A.S.Sū. 12/74-75*
	Granthi	*Vākucī Vividha Yoga*	*A.S.K. 49/78*
	Granthi	*Guggula Vividha Yoga*	*A.S.U. 49/171*
	Granthi	*Śiva Gutikā*	*A.S.U. 49/193*
41.	*Arbuda*	*Vākucī Vividha Yoga*	*A.S.U. 49/78*
	Arbuda	*Śivā Gutikā*	*A.S.U. 49/193*
42.	*Ślipada*	*Pippalī Vardhamāna Rasāyana*	*A.S.Ci. 12/13*
	Ślipada	*Vacā Ghṛta*	*A.S.U. 49/99*
	Ślipada	*Śiva Gutikā*	*A.S.U. 49/193*
	Ślipada	*Vṛdha Drākṣā Yoga*	*A.S.U. 49/214*
43.	*Apaci*	*Guggula*	*A.S.Sū. 12/75*
	Apaci	*Guggula Vividha Yoga*	*A.S.U. 49/171*
	Apaci	*Vṛdha Drākṣā Vividha Yoga*	*A.S.U. 49/213*
44.	*Yoni Roga*	*Śirīṣa Taila*	*A.S.U. 10/17*
	Yoni Roga	*Guggula Vividha Yoga*	*A.S.U. 49/160-178*
45.	*Śukra Doṣa*	*Śirīṣa Taila*	*A.S.U. 10/17*
	Śukra Doṣa	*Cayavanaprāśa*	*A.S.U. 49/29*
	Sukra Doṣa	*Guggula Vividha Yoga*	*A.S.U. 49/170*
	Śukra Doṣa	*Śivā Gutikā*	*A.S.U. 49/193*
46.	*Viṣa*	*Suvarṅa*	*A.S.Sū. 12/12*
	Viṣa	*Śivā Gutikā*	*A.S.U. 49/193*
	Viṣa	*Śirīṣa Taila*	*A.S.U. 10/17*

	Viṣa	*Brāhmī Vacādi Yoga*	*A.S.U. 49/46*
	Viṣa	*Vākucī Vividha Yoga*	*A.S.U. 49/95*
	Viṣa	*Somāmṛta Ghṛta*	*A.S.U. 49/158*
	Viṣa	*Śilājatu Vividha Yoga*	*A.S.U. 49/190*
	Viṣa	*Suvarṅa Mākṣika Yoga*	*A.S.U. 49/199*
	Viṣa	*Vṛdha Drākṣā Vividha Yoga*	*A.S.U. 49/213*
47.	*Āmavāta*	*Vṛdha Drākṣā Vividha Yoga*	*A.S.U. 49/214*
48.	*Kāmlā*	*Amṛtā*	*A.S.Sū. 12/71*
	Kāmlā	*Śivā Gutikā*	*A.S.U. 49/193*
49.	*Halimaka*	*Śivā Gutikā*	*A.S.U. 49/193*
50.	*Ānāha*	*Śivā Gutikā*	*A.S.U. 49/193*
51.	*Urustambha*	*Śivā Gutikā*	*A.S.U. 49/193*
	Urustambha	*Ālambuśa Prayoga*	*A.S.U. 49/75*
52.	*Gala Ganda*	*Pippalī Vardhamāna Rasāyana*	*A.S.U. 49/73*
	Gala Ganda	*Guggulu*	*A.S.Sū. 12/75*
53.	*Twaka Roga*	*Triphalā Rasāyana*	*A.S.Sū. 12/47*
	Twaka Roga	*Vakucī Vividha Yoga*	*A.S.U. 49/78*
	Twaka Roga	*Kancukī Vividha Yoga*	*A.S.U. 49/152*
	Twaka Roga	*Suvarṅa Mākṣika*	*A.S.U. 49/199*
	Twaka Roga	*Vṛdha Drakṣā Vividha Yoga*	*A.S.U. 49/216*

54.	*Bhrama*	*Dugdha*	*A.S.Sū. 6/55*
	Bhrama	*Nāgabalā Ghṛta*	*A.S.Ci. 5/75*
55.	*Medo Roga*	*Triphalā Rasāyana*	*A.S.Sū. 12/47*
	Medo Roga	*Bhallātaka Vividha Yoga*	*A.S.U. 49/58*
	Medo Roga	*Vidanga Vividha Yoga*	*A.S.U. 49/74*
	Medo Roga	*Guggulu Vividha Yoga*	*A.S.U. 49/169*
	Medo Roga	*Śilājatu Vividha Yoga*	*A.S.U. 49/189*
56.	*Dāha*	*Nāgabalā Ghṛta*	*A.S.Ci. 5/75*
	Dāha	*Amṛta*	*A.S.Sū. 12/71*
57.	*Pālitya, Khālitya*	*Nāgabalā Ghṛta*	*A.S.Ci. 5/75*
	Pālitya, Khālitya	*Agastya Leha*	*A.S.Ci. 5/86*
	Pālitya, Khālitya	*Śivā Gutikā*	*A.S.U. 49/193*
58.	*Arucī*	*Agastya Leha*	*A.S.Ci. 5/87*
	Arucī	*Yogarāja Rasāyana*	*A.S.Ci. 21/14*
	Arucī	*Śivā Gutikā*	*A.S.U. 49/193*
59.	*Moha*	*Mustādi Yāpna Vasti*	*A.S.K. 5/11*
	Moha	*Guggula Vividha Yoga*	*A.S.U. 49/170*
60.	*Vivandha*	*Gambhārī*	*A.S.Sū. 7/178*
	Vivandha	*Bhallātaka Vividha Yoga*	*A.S.U. 49/58*

61. Aśmarī	*Mustādi Yāpnā Vasti*	*A.S.K.*	*5/11*
Aśmarī	*Vākuci Vividha Yoga*	*A.S.U.*	*49/78*
Aśmarī	*Silājatu Vividha Yoga*	*A.S.U.*	*49/190*

Note : *A* = *Aṣṭānga*
S = *Sangraha*
Sū = *Sūtra*
Ci = *Cikitsā*
U = *Uttara tantra*
K = *Kalpa sthāna*

Chapter IX

Rasāyana Described in *Aṣṭānga Hṛdya*

Single *Rasāyana* Drugs Described in *Aṣṭānga Hṛdya*

S.N.	*Rasāyana Dravya*	References
1.	*Godugdha*	*A.H.Sū. 5/22-23*
2.	*Kākamācī*	*A.H.Sū. 6/73*
3.	*Vidāri Kanda*	*A.H.Sū. 6/85*
4.	*Kāśamarī*	*A.H.Sū. 6/122*
5.	*Pippalī*	*A.H.Sū. 6/162*
6.	*Tuvaraka*	*A.H.Ci. 19/53*
7.	*Bhallātaka*	*A.H.Ci. 19/53*
8.	*Vākucī*	*A.H.Ci. 19/53*
9.	*Citrakamūla*	*A.H.Ci. 19/53*
10.	*Śilājatu*	*A.H.Ci. 19/53*
11.	*Guggulu*	*A.H.Ci. 22/64-65*
12.	*Lahasuna*	*A.H.Ci. 22/70*
13.	*Jala*	*A.H.U. 39/145*
14.	*Madhu*	*A.H.U. 39/145*
15.	*Ghṛta*	*A.H.U. 39/145*
16.	*Haritakī*	*A.H.U. 39/147*

17.	*Punarnavā*	*A.H.U. 39/154*
18.	*Mūrvā*	*A.H.U. 39/155*
19.	*Bṛhatī*	*A.H.U. 39/155*
20.	*Śālaparṇī*	*A.H.U. 39/155*
21.	*Balā*	*A.H.U. 39/155*
22.	*Uśira*	*A.H.U. 39/155*
23.	*Pathā*	*A.H.U. 39/155*
24.	*Asana*	*A.H.U. 39/155*
25.	*Sārīvā*	*A.H.U. 39/155*
26.	*Agaru*	*A.H.U. 39/155*
27.	*Tagara*	*A.H.U. 39/155*
28.	*Aśwagandhā*	*A.H.U. 39/157*
29.	*Candana*	*A.H.U. 39/155*
30.	*Kṛṣṇa Tila*	*A.H.U. 39/158*
31.	*Bhṛngaraja*	*A.H.U. 39/162*
32.	*Vacā*	*A.H.U. 39/163*

Note : *A* = *Aṣṭānga*

H = *Hṛdya*

Sū = *Sūtra*

Ci = *Cikitsā*

U = *Uttara Tantra*

Rasāyana Yoga Described in Aṣṭānga Hṛdya

SN.	*Rasāyana . Yoga*	Reference
1.	*Triphalā*	*A.H.Sū. 6/159*
2.	*Pippalī Vardhamāna Rasāyana*	*A.H.U. 39/98-100*
3.	*Vaśiṣṭa Haritakī*	*A.H.Ci. 3/133-140*
4.	*Elādi Ghṛta*	*A.H.Ci. 5/28-32*
5.	*Śilājatu Rasāyana*	*A.H.Ci. 12/34-35*
6.	*Brāhma Rasāyana*	*A.H.U. 39/15-23*
7.	*Āmalakī Rasāyana*	*A.H.U. 39/28-32*
8.	*Agastya Haritakī*	*A.H.Ci. 3/127-132*
9.	*Triphalādi Rasāyana*	*A.H.U. 39/43*
10.	*Balā Taila*	*A.H.Ci. 22/45-46*
11.	*Brahma Prāśa Rasāyana*	*A.H.U. 39/15-23*
12.	*Haritakyādi Rasāyana*	*A.H.U. 39/24-27*
13.	*Āmalkī Rasāyana*	*A.H.U. 39/28-32*
14.	*Cayavana Prāśa Avleha*	*A.H.U. 39/33-41*
15.	*Triphalā Rasāyana*	*A.H.U. 39/42-43*
16.	*Medhā Vardhaka Rasāyana*	*A.H.U. 39/44-45*
17.	*Pancārvinda Ghṛta*	*A.H.U. 39/48*
18.	*Catuṣku Balya Ghṛta*	*A.H.U. 39/49*
19.	*Brāhmī Ādi Rasāyana Yoga*	*A.H.U. 39/50-53*
20.	*Nagabalā Rasāyana*	*A.H.U. 39/54-55*
21.	*Gokṣaru Rasāyana*	*A.H.U. 39/56-57*
22.	*Vārāhī Kanda Rasāyana*	*A.H.U. 39/58*
23.	*Vārāhī Kanda Ghṛta*	*A.H.U. 39/59*
24.	*Vidarī Kandādi Rasāyana Yoga*	*A.H.U. 39/60-61*

25. *Citraka Rasāyana* *A.H.U. 39/62-65*
26. *Bhallātaka Rasāyana Yoga* *A.H.U. 39/66-71*
27. *Anya Bhallātaka Rasāyana* *A.H.U. 39/72-74*
28. *Amṛta Bhallātaka Pāka* *A.H.U. 39/75-78*
29. *Bhallātaka Taila* *A.H.U. 39/79*
30. *Bhallātaka Yoga* *A.H.U. 39/80-82*
31. *Kuṣṭhanāśaka Tuvraka RasāyanaA.H.U. 39/84-89*
32. *Tuvaraka Taila Rasāyana* *A.H.U. 39/94-95*
33. *Pippalī Rasāyana* *A.H.U. 39/96-97*
34. *Śunṭhayādi Anya Yoga* *A.H.U. 39/104-105*
35. *Lahaśuna Rasāyana Yoga* *A.H.U. 39/111-129*
36. *Āmalakī Rasāyana* *A.H.U. 39/148-149*
37. *Lohādi Yoga* *A.H.U. 39/150*
38. *Vidangādi Rasāyana* *A.H.U. 39/151*
39. *Āmalakayādi Yoga* *A.H.U. 39/148-149*
40. *Khadira Bhāvita Triphala GhṛtaA.H.U. 39/152*
41. *Bījaka Sarkarā yoga* *A.H.U. 39/153*
42. *Śatāvarī Ghṛta* *A.H.U. 39/156*
43. *Gokṣurādi Yoga* *A.H.U. 39/159*
44. *Āmalakī Tilādi Yoga* *A.H.U. 39/160-161*
45. *Śilājatwādi Yoga* *A.H.U. 39/161*
46. *Mandūkaparṅī* *A.H.U. 39/164*
47. *Langlyādi Yoga* *A.H.U. 39/165-168*
48. *Nārsingha Ghṛta* *A.H.U. 39/170-173*
49. *Nārsingha Taila* *A.H.U. 39/176*
50. *Vāta Raktādi Yāpnā Vasti* *A.H.K. 4/37-42*

51.	*Mādhu Tailika Vasti*	A.H.K. 4/27-28
52.	*Godhādi Mānsa Vasti*	A.H.K. 4/49-52
53.	*Śatapāka Sahastra Pāka Balā Taila*	A.H.Ci. 22/45-46
54.	*Abhāyāmalaki Rasāyana*	A.H.Ci. 22/64-65

Note : *A* = *Aṣṭānga*
H = *Hṛdya*
Sū = *Sūtra*
Ci = *Cikitsā*
K = *Kalpa Sthāna*
U = *Uttara Tantra*

Rasāyana **Therapy Indicated in Various Disorders in *Aṣṭānga Hṛdya***

S.N.	Disorders	*Rasāyana* Used	References
1.	*Jwara*	*Godugdha*	*A.H.Sū. 5/22*
	Jwara	*Agastya Harītakī*	*A.H.Ci. 3/127-132*
	Jwara	*Vāta Raktādi Yāpnā Vasti*	*A.H.K. 4/37-42*
2.	*Raktā Pitta*	*Godugdha*	*A.H.Sū 5/22*
3.	*Kāsa*	*Godugdha*	*A.H.Sū. 5/22*
4.	*Śwāsa*	*Godugdha*	*A.H.Sū. 5/22*
	Śwāsa	*Pippalī*	*A.H.Sū. 6/162*
	Śwāsa	*Agastya Harītakī*	*A.H.Ci. 3/127-132*
5.	*Rājayakṣmā*	*Agastya Harītakī*	*A.H.Ci. 3/27-132*
	Rājayakṣmā	*Eladi Ghṛta*	*A.H.Ci. 5/28-32*
6.	*Hṛdroga*	*Agastya Harītakī*	*A.H.Ci. 3/127-132*
7.	*Tṛṣṇā*	*Godugdha*	*A.H.Sū. 5/22*
8.	*Arśa*	*Agastya Harītakī*	*A.H.Ci. 3/127-32*
	Arśa	*Madhu Tailika Vasti*	*A.H.K. 4/27-28*
	Arśa	*Vāta Raktādi Yāpnā Vasti*	*A.H.K. 4/37-42*
9.	*Grahaṇī*	*Agastya Harītakī*	*A.H.Ci. 3/127-132*
10.	*Mutrakṛchra*	*Godugdha*	*A.H.Su. 5/22*
11.	*Prameha*	*Agastya Harītakī*	*A.H.Ci. 3/127-132*
	Prameha	*Elādi Ghṛta*	*A.H.Ci. 5/28-32*
	Prameha	*Mādhu Tailika Vasti*	*A.H.K. 4/27-28*
	Prameha	*Vāta Raktādi Yāpna Vasti*	*A.H.K. 4/37-42*

12.	*Gulma*	*Agastya Harītaki.*	*A.H.Ci. 3/127-32*
	Gulma	*Elādi Ghṛta*	*A.H.Ci. 5/28-32*
	Gulma	*Madhu Tailika Vasti*	*A.H.K. 4/27-28*
	Gulma	*Vāta Raktādi Yāpnā Vasti*	*A.H.K. 4/37-42*
13.	*Udara Roga*	*Pippali Vardhamāna Rasāyana*	*A.H.U. 39/98-100*
14.	*Pravāhikā*	*Vāta Raktādi Yāpnā Vasti*	*A.H.K. 4/37-42*
15.	*Ādhmāna*	*Vāta Raktādi Yāpnā Vasti*	*A.H.K. 4/37-42*
16.	*Śiraha Śula*	*Vāta Raktādi Yāpnā Vasti*	*A.H.K. 4/37-42*
17.	*Karṅa Śula*	*Vāta Raktādi Yāpnā Vasti*	*A.H.K. 4/37-42*
18.	*Asṛgdara*	*Vāta Raktādi Yāpnā Vasti*	*A.H.K. 4/37-42*
19.	*Unmāda*	*Vāta Raktādi Yāpnā Vasti*	*A.H.K. 4/37-42*
20.	*Aśmarī*	*Vāta Raktadi Yapnā Vasti*	*A.H.K. 4/37-42*
21.	*Vasti Kundlikā*	*Vāta Raktādi Yāpnā Vasti*	*A.H.K. 4/37-42*

Note : *A* = *Aṣṭānga*
H = *Hṛdya*
Sū = *Sūtra*
Ci = *Cikitsā*
U = *Uttara Tantra*
K = *Kalpa Sthāna*

Bibliography

* Ankad, Vishwanāth; Sharma, A.K. (Supervisor) Conceptual and Clinical Evaluation of Rasāyana Therapy with special reference to Āmalkī Rasāyana, M.D. (Ay.) Thesis, P.G. Deptt. of Kāyacikitsā, N.I.A. Jaipur, 2000.
* Ācārya Yadavji Trikamji : Caraka Samhitā-Cakrapaṅī Tikā, published by Kāshi Sanskrit Grantha Mala, Vārānasi, 4th edition, 1998.
* *Ācārya*, Dalhaṅa : Suśruta Samhitā, Published by Chaukhamba Orientalia, Vārānasi, 3rd edition, 1997.
* Addhamala : Śārangadhara Samhitā with Dīpikā Commentary, published by Chaukhamba Sanskrit Series-Vārānasi, 2nd edition, 1998.
* Awasthi Chandra Shekhar; Sharma, Madan Gopal; Āyurvediya Rasāyana Tantra; M.D. (Ay.) Thesis, P.G. Deptt of Kāyacikitsā, National Institute of Āyurveda, 1987.
* Chavan Santosh; Sharma, A.K. (Supervisor) : Studies on Aging and Rasāyana Effect of Aśwagandhā (Withania somnifera) in elderly persons, M.D. (Ay.) Thesis, P.G. Deptt of Kāyacikitsā, N.I.A. Jaipur, 2000.
* Gupta, Atri Dev : Aṣṭānga Hṛdaya-Vidyotini Tikā, Published by Chaukhamba Sanskrit Sansthana-Vārānasi 1st edition, 2000.

* Gupta, Atri Dev; Suśruta-Samhitā, Published by Moti Lal Banarasi Das, Delhi, 5th edition, 1975.

* Kunte, Anna Moreshwar, Aṣṭānga Hṛdya with Sarwānga Sunehi & Āyurvediya Rasāyana Vyākhyā, Published by Krishna Das Āyurveda Series-4, 1st edition, 1997.

* Khunt, Chandresh U; Singh Gurdeep : Studies on Kutiprāveśika & Vātātapika Rasāyana effects of Vārāhi Kanda in promotion of health & management of Aging, Deptt. of Kāyacikitsā, Ph.D. Thesis, Gujrāta Āyurveda University, Jāmnagar, Aug. 2003.

* Kahalekar Dhananjaya; Shandilya M.K., Evaluation of Rejuvenation effect of Āmalkī (Emblica officinalis) in old age, P.G. Deptt of Kāya Cikitsā, M.D. (Ay.) Thesis, National Institute of Āyurveda, Jaipur, 1999.

* Murthy, Srikanta K.R.; Aṣṭānga Samgraha of Vāgabhatta English Translation, Published by Chaukhamba Orientalia Vārānasi, 1st edition, 1996.

* Mishra Bhāva, Bhāva Prakaśa II Part, Published by Chaukhamba Sanskrit Sansthāna-Vārānasi 5th edition 1998.

* Pandeya, Kaśi Nāth : Caraka Samhitā-Vidyotani Tikā Published by Chaukhamba Bhārti Academy-Vārānasi, 22nd edition, 1986.

* Pāthaka, Mohana Lal, Rasāyana Evaṁ Vājikaraṅa Vivecana, Published by Nidhi Prakāśana, Sunāmi Gate Patiyalā, 2nd edition, 1995.

* Śastri, Ambika Dutta : Suśruta Samhitā Āyurveda Tatwa Sandīpikā Tikā, Published by Chaukhamba Sanskrit Sansthāna-Vārānansi 11th edition, 1997.

* Sharma, R.K.; Das, Bhagwan; Caraka Samhitā, English translation, Published by Chaukhamba Sanskrit Series Office, Vārānasi, 6th edition, 1999.

* Sharma, A.K. and Singh, R.H. (Supervisor), Clinical and Biological Studies on the Role of Amṛta Bhallātaka as a Naimittika Rasāyana in the Management of Āmavata (R.A.), M.D. (Ay.) Thesis, Banāras Hindu University, Vārānasi,1980

* Sharma, A.K. and Singh, R.H. (Supervisor) : Rasāyana-Vajikaraṅa (Śāstriya Evama Vaigyanika Adhyayana), Ph.D. Thesis, K.S.D.S. University, Darbhanga, 1986.

* Sharma, A.K., The Pancakarma Treatment of Āyurveda including Keraliya Pancakarma, Sri Satguru Publications, Delhi, 2002.

* Singh, R.H. and Udupa, K.N: Rejuvenation Therapy, In Science and Philosophy of Indian Medicine, Baidyanātha Āyurveda Bhawan, Nagpur, 1978.

* Singh, R.H. : Medhya Rasāyana: Bulletin of Indian Medicine, Banāras Hindu University, Vārānasi,1976.

* Singh, R.H: Āyurvediya Nidāna Cikitsā Ke Siddhānta, I part, I Edn., Chaukhamba Publications, Vārānasi. 1982.

* Singh, R.H. and Shukla, M.P, : Elements of Rasāyana Therapy in Śarangadhara Samhitā, Nagarjuna, 19, 7/5, 1976.

* Singh, R.H. : Clinical Studies on the Anti-Anxiety Effect of Some Indigenous Drugs (1978) Quart J. Surges, Sec. Vol. 14, 1978

* Singh, R.H. : Kāya Cikitsā in 2 volumes, Chaukhamba Publication, Vārānasi, 1994.

* Singh, R.H. : Rasāyana and Vājīkaraṅa (Promotive Therapy) : In History of medicine in India : Ed. by Sharma P.V., Indian National Science Academy, New Delhi, 1992.

* Singh, R.H. : The Holistic Principles of Ayurvedic Medicine, Chaukhamba Publication, Vārānasi, 1998.

* Shastri, Sudarshana : Madhava Nidana Published by Chaukhamba Sanskrit Sansthana, Vārānasi, 27th edition, 1998.

* Srivastava, Shailja : Śārangdhara Samhitā—'Jiwanaprada' Hindi Commentary, Published by Chaukhamba Orientalia, Vārānasi, Ist edition, 1996.

* Shastri, Brahma Shankara : Bhāva Prakāśa-Vidyotani Hindi Commentary, Published by Chaukhamba Sanskrita Sansthana, Vārānasi 8th edition, 1997.

* Srivastava, Shailja : Ayurvediya Rasāyana Sara, Published by Chaukhamba Orientalia, Vārānasi, Ist edition, 2000.

* Tripathi, Ravidutta, Aṣṭānga Hṛdya-'Saroj' Tīkā, Published by Chaukhmaba Sanskrit Pratisthana, Delhi, 1996.

* Tripathi, Indradeva : Cakradutta—'Vidya Prabha' Tikā, Published by Chaukhamba Sanskrit Sansthana, Vārānasi, 4th edition, 2002.

* Tripathi, Indradeva : Yoga Ratnākara—Vidyotani Hindi Commentary, Published by Krishna Das Academy, Vārānasi, Ist edition, 1998.

* Upādhyāya, Om Prakāsh : Rasāyana—Vājikaraṅa Darpaṅa, Published & Distributed by Alok Upādhyāya, Jaipur, 1st edition, 2003.